ASSESSING
UNSTOPPABLE
LEARNING

TOM HIERCK   ANGELA FREESE

Edited by Douglas Fisher and Nancy Frey

Solution Tree | Press

a division of
Solution Tree

555 North Morton Street
Bloomington, IN 47404
800.733.6786 (toll free) / 812.336.7700
FAX: 812.336.7790

email: info@SolutionTree.com
SolutionTree.com

Visit **go.SolutionTree.com/assessment** to download the free reproducibles in this book.

Printed in the United States of America

21 20 19 18 17   1 2 3 4 5

Library of Congress Cataloging-in-Publication Data

Names: Hierck, Tom, 1960- author. | Freese, Angela, author.
Title: Assessing unstoppable learning / Tom Hierck, Angela Freese ; edited by
   Douglas Fisher and Nancy Frey.
Description: Bloomington, IN : Solution Tree Press, 2017. | Includes
   bibliographical references and index.
Identifiers: LCCN 2017015291 | ISBN 9781943874231 (perfect bound)
Subjects: LCSH: Educational evaluation. | Educational tests and measurements.
   | Curriculum planning.
Classification: LCC LB2822.75 .H54 2017 | DDC 371.26--dc23 LC record available at https://lccn.loc
.gov/2017015291

Solution Tree
Jeffrey C. Jones, CEO
Edmund M. Ackerman, President

Solution Tree Press
President and Publisher: Douglas M. Rife
Editorial Director: Sarah Payne-Mills
Managing Production Editor: Caroline Cascio
Senior Production Editor: Tara Perkins
Senior Editor: Amy Rubenstein
Copy Editor: Jessi Finn
Text and Cover Designer: Laura Cox
Editorial Assistants: Jessi Finn and Kendra Slayton

As I reflect on my name appearing on a sixteenth book, I am humbled by the good fortune that has come my way and honored by the encouragement I have received to make this all possible. Beginning with a family support system of my wife Ingrid, our three kids and their spouses, plus our six grandbabies (including the newest addition, Bodhi), through friends and local colleagues, to the many acquaintances I have made in my travels, I am a fortunate man. This book is not possible without your backing. Additionally, I'd like to dedicate this book to the memory of my sister-in-law, Heide Jozwik, who lost her battle with cancer. Like many of our colleagues, she was a student-centered educator who strived to make a difference each day and whose loss will be felt most by the kids she inspired.

— Tom

To my daughter Kennedy—your tenacious pursuit of why and your insatiable love for learning inspire me to keep learning, reflecting, and growing as a mother and an educator every day. You are my everything, and you make my heart so happy!

And to my late grandmother, Darlene—although her dynamic career as a first-grade teacher and principal spanned almost five decades, she still knew all the names of each of her students, and ultimately their kids' names, and even their grandkids' names. May her legacy of building relationships, inspiring hope and perseverance, and fostering a love of learning in each of her students serve as inspiration to all of us. I can only hope to be half the educator she was.

— Angie

Acknowledgments

Although our names appear on the cover, this book would not be possible without the support and input of many colleagues and friends.

Beginning with the Solution Tree family, we would like to thank the following key supporters. Douglas Rife has been a visionary in his role as publisher, and his support has been invaluable. Claudia Wheatley brought the two of us together, knowing our styles and abilities would mesh to create a high-quality book. We hope you'll validate her faith in us. Jeff Jones has built a company that encourages educators to find their voice and share that with colleagues. His commitment to educators through books and events is unparalleled in our field. Amy Rubenstein was our first editor and key support person, and we thank her for the initial shaping of this text. Tara Perkins became our go-to person for all of the subsequent edits, and her suggestions ensured that our ideas blended and led to a cohesive text. We are fortunate to get the opportunity to share our thoughts in the words of this book and to follow that with the opportunity to share this work through professional learning opportunities coordinated by Shannon Ritz and her PD team. Our Assessment Center colleagues will see their fingerprints in various places in this book. In particular, we are grateful to Cassandra Erkens, Tom Schimmer, and Nicole Vagle for their contributions.

At the outset of the writing and throughout the process, we were supported by insightful feedback, shared narratives, and exemplars provided by colleagues. Trailblazers like Charlie Coleman, Garth Larson, Michael McDowell, Sue Stephenson, Pam Bloom, Erika Fisher, Scott Greseth, Michelle Hicks, and Denise Pontrelli are paving the way with their innovation and collaboration to serve as exemplars to catapult this work forward. Like all educators, they have full plates and yet made the time to provide timely feedback and share some content.

We are very appreciative of the opportunity to write a book driven by the high-quality work of Douglas Fisher and Nancy Frey. They have charted new territory with *Unstoppable Learning* and were generous in their time and support as we crafted this book.

Finally, thanks to the thousands of educators and students we've been fortunate to interact with over the years. Your sharing of successes and failures reminds us of the great work that has been done and the remaining work that lies before us.

Solution Tree Press would like to thank the following reviewers:

Jennifer Adams
Assessment Coordinator
Arlington Heights School District 25
Arlington Heights, Illinois

Elizabeth Gaffney
Academic Coach
Secondary English Language Arts
 Curriculum Specialist
Chandler Unified School District
Chandler, Arizona

Peter Glahn
Principal
Timberline Middle School
Alpine, Utah

Paula Maeker
Educational Consultant
Spring, Texas

Cody Mothershead
Principal
White River High School
Buckley, Washington

Stacie Stanley
Director of Curriculum, Instruction,
 and Support Services
Burnsville-Eagan-Savage
 School District 191
Burnsville, Minnesota

Visit **go.SolutionTree.com/assessment** to
download the free reproducibles in this book.

Table of Contents

Reproducible pages are in italics.

About the Editors

 **Douglas Fisher, PhD,** is professor of educational leadership at San Diego State University and a teacher leader at Health Sciences High and Middle College. He teaches courses in instructional improvement and formative assessment. As a classroom teacher, Fisher focuses on English language arts instruction. He was director of professional development for the City Heights Educational Collaborative and also taught English at Hoover High School.

Fisher received an International Reading Association Celebrate Literacy Award for his work on literacy leadership. For his work as codirector of the City Heights Professional Development Schools, Fisher received the Christa McAuliffe Award. He was corecipient of the Farmer Award for excellence in writing from the National Council of Teachers of English (NCTE) as well as the 2014 Exemplary Leader for the Conference on English Leadership, also from the NCTE.

Fisher has written numerous articles on reading and literacy, differentiated instruction, and curriculum design. His books include *Teaching Students to Read Like Detectives*, *Checking for Understanding*, *Better Learning Through Structured Teaching*, and *Rigorous Reading*.

He earned a bachelor's degree in communication, a master's degree in public health, an executive master's degree in business, and a doctoral degree in multicultural education. Fisher completed postdoctoral study at the National Association of State Boards of Education focused on standards-based reforms.

Nancy Frey, PhD, is a professor of educational leadership at San Diego State University. She teaches courses on professional development, systems change, and instructional approaches for supporting students with diverse learning needs. Frey also teaches classes at Health Sciences High and Middle College in San Diego. She is a credentialed special educator, reading specialist, and administrator in California.

Before joining the university faculty, Frey was a public school teacher in Florida. She worked at the state level for the Florida Inclusion Network, helping districts design systems for supporting students with disabilities in general education classrooms.

She is the recipient of the 2008 Early Career Achievement Award from the Literacy Research Association and the Christa McAuliffe Award for excellence in teacher education from the American Association of State Colleges and Universities. She was corecipient of the Farmer Award for excellence in writing from the National Council of Teachers of English for the article "Using Graphic Novels, Anime, and the Internet in an Urban High School."

Frey is coauthor of *Text-Dependent Questions*, *Using Data to Focus Instructional Improvement*, and *Text Complexity: Raising Rigor in Reading*. She has written articles for the *Reading Teacher*, *Journal of Adolescent and Adult Literacy*, *English Journal*, *Voices From the Middle*, *Middle School Journal*, *Remedial and Special Education*, and *Educational Leadership*.

To book Douglas Fisher or Nancy Frey for professional development, contact pd@SolutionTree.com.

About the Authors

Tom Hierck has been an educator since 1983 and has held a variety of roles, including teacher, department head, vice principal, principal, director of international programs, sessional university instructor, Ministry of Education project coordinator, and assistant superintendent. This has allowed him the opportunity to see education from a myriad of perspectives that are reflected in his writing.

Hierck is a compelling presenter, infusing his message of hope with strategies culled from the real world. He has presented to schools and districts across North America and overseas with a message of celebration for educators seeking to make a difference in students' lives. Hierck's dynamic presentations explore the importance of being purpose driven in creating positive learning environments and a positive school culture, responding to the behavioral and academic needs of students, and utilizing assessment to improve student learning. His belief that "every student is a success story waiting to be told" has led him to work with teachers and administrators to create the kinds of learning environments that are effective for all educators while building strong relationships that facilitate learning for all students.

Hierck was a recipient of the Queen's Golden Jubilee Medallion, presented by the premier and lieutenant governor of British Columbia, for being a recognized leader in the field of public education. Hierck earned a master's degree at Gonzaga University and a bachelor's degree and teacher certification at the University of British Columbia.

This is the eighth Solution Tree title bearing Hierck's name, with number nine in the production phase. He contributed to *The Teacher as Assessment Leader* and *The Principal as Assessment Leader*, coauthored the best-selling books *Pyramid of Behavior Interventions: Seven Keys to a Positive Learning Environment* and *Starting a Movement: Building Culture From the Inside Out in Professional Learning Communities*, and coauthored *Uniting Academic and Behavior Interventions: Solving the Skill or Will Dilemma* and *Strategies for Mathematics Instruction and Intervention, 6–8*. His first solo effort, *Seven Keys to a Positive Learning Environment in Your Classroom* was published in 2017.

To learn more about Tom Hierck's work, visit www.tomhierck.com or follow @thierck on Twitter.

Angela Freese is the director of research, assessment, and accountability for Osseo Area Public Schools in Maple Grove, Minnesota. Her work enables her to promote systems thinking via collaborative structures that highlight the marriage of curriculum, assessment, and instruction within a learning organization. She has also facilitated work with instructional coaches and curriculum-support teachers to bring the *what* and the *how* of learning together for teachers and administrators. She was previously a middle school assistant principal in the North St. Paul-Maplewood-Oakdale School District in Minnesota and an elementary school assistant principal for Rochester Public Schools in Rochester, Minnesota. Her administrative experiences have taken place in schools with highly diverse student populations. Freese has developed high-impact collaborative teams focused on high levels of learning for both staff and students, positive cultures, and curriculum-instruction-assessment models that focus on engaging students as partners in the learning process.

Freese was an implementation associate at the Office of Curriculum and Instruction for Rochester Public Schools. Her focus was on developing and revising coherent district curriculum and instructional strategies aligned with district, state, and national standards. She supported teachers and administrators in curriculum mapping, pacing, and instructional alignment and promoted the use of consistent instructional frameworks and research-based strategies. She analyzed district and site data to improve curriculum and instruction, developed and implemented curricular and instructional processes, and provided coaching and staff development to classroom teachers and district instructional staff.

She has extensive experience in staff development design and implementation. As a key player in instructional alignment projects, Freese collaboratively designed and implemented ongoing, job-embedded staff development opportunities for hundreds of administrators and teachers across various schools and districts. Freese also designed and implemented a plan that enabled building administrators to further their capacity as assessment leaders.

Freese earned a bachelor of arts degree in elementary education at Luther College and a master of arts degree in elementary education at Saint Mary's University of Minnesota. She became a licensed principal and was also certified in professional development at the University of Minnesota.

To book Tom Hierck or Angela Freese for professional development, contact pd@SolutionTree.com.

Foreword

By Douglas Fisher and Nancy Frey

We have spent the past several decades trying to figure out ways to help teachers decide *what to teach* and *how to teach it*. In other words, we are in search of the links between curriculum (what to teach) and instruction (how to teach it), which we see as two sides of the same coin. Assessment is the key that guides teachers as they grapple with answering the question of what they will teach and how. Before we discuss that, however, it's important to consider the influences on curriculum and instruction beyond assessments. Yes, assessment data should guide teachers' curriculum and instruction, but there are other factors at play.

There have been any number of curriculum wars as various groups attempt to influence what students learn in school. Examples of these curriculum debate topics range from phonics to evolution. Members of the public, especially through standards-setting boards, have profound sway on what gets taught in school. This is both good and bad. We do think that there should be appropriately rigorous expectations for students and that the curriculum needs to ensure that students develop a range of skills and strategies. We also believe that teachers can use assessments to identify the gap between what students already know and can do, and what they still need to learn. This gap is where the content, or curriculum, students need to experience resides.

But the official curriculum is only part of the story. Most political debates are about the official curriculum, but teachers need to think of curriculum in a more expansive way. George Posner (2004) notes that there are at least five aspects to the curriculum:

1. The *official* curriculum, or written curriculum, gives the basic lesson plan teachers are to follow, including objectives, sequence, and materials. This provides the basis for accountability.

xvi ASSESSING UNSTOPPABLE LEARNING

2. The *operational* curriculum is what the teacher teaches in class and how he or she communicates; this curriculum includes the learning outcomes for the student.

3. The *hidden* curriculum includes the norms and values of the surrounding society. These are stronger and more durable than the first two aspects, and may be in conflict with them.

4. The *null* curriculum consists of what is not taught. Educators must consider the reasons why things are not included in the official or operational curriculum.

5. The *extra* curriculum includes the planned experiences outside of the specific educational session.

The other side of the coin is instruction, or how students will learn the content that will close the gap. There are far fewer political debates about instruction, and teachers are generally able to plan learning experiences for students. Of course, the amount of freedom teachers have to select instructional routines has varied from decade to decade. For example, in the world of reading, the 1990s were marked by scripted and prescriptive approaches to instruction (as well as expected fidelity to a specific curriculum). As we write this foreword, there is a loosening of these expectations, and an increase in the expectation that teachers exercise their professional judgement in deciding how to engage their students in meaningful learning experiences.

Having said that, we are not suggesting that teachers choose randomly from a set of instructional routines and strategies. Instructional decisions should be guided by data. Some of the data can come from educational research. Teachers should know which instructional approaches are more likely than others to ensure that students learn. This is a good starting place for selecting strategies, but it is not the only place. Teachers should use assessment data to determine if the instructional approaches they have selected have impacted students' learning. If they have, great. If not, then teachers should change their approach. Teachers should never be so enamored with an instructional approach that they continue to use it, even in the face of assessment data that indicate a lack of learning.

See, assessment is the driver that teachers can use to ensure that students learn and that learning becomes unstoppable. Assessments should guide the decisions that teachers make about both the curriculum and the instruction, and those decisions should ensure that students achieve at high levels. That's why we appreciate this book so much. Tom Hierck and Angela Freese have provided us with a systematic approach to collecting and using assessment data that can guide these very important decisions that teachers need to make. When implemented, the ideas that Hierck and Freese suggest guarantee that students learn and that teachers can exercise their professional expertise in collaboration with their colleagues. But even more important, when strong assessment systems are in place, students assume increased responsibility for their own learning and learn beyond the walls of the classroom. And isn't that our collective goal—that students learn on their own for the rest of their lives?

Introduction

*We can't solve problems by using the same
kind of thinking we used when we created them.*

—Albert Einstein

Stories have undeniable power. Storytelling is deeply embedded in all human cultures and has a profound influence on how we think, how we dream, and how we live our lives through the lens of what we have grown to value most. As teachers, we all have our favorite story to share—a memory, a lesson to learn, a legend. Some story lines have remained true, and others have evolved, or we have embellished them to support new and unique circumstances. Retelling these stories honors the knowledge and experience of those who came before us and helps create a strong, sustainable future.

Think back to your schooling experience. What stories do you remember most? We anticipate that you can quickly recall good times with friends, moments of inspiration and empowerment from your favorite teachers, and points of pride and accomplishment. We also imagine that you—with the same crystal clarity—can recall struggles and complications with friends, times of discouragement with teachers, and moments when you tripped and fell along the way. While our experiences shape the stories that we tell our friends and family, they also shape the manner in which we approach our work. What moments from your educational journey do you aspire to replicate with your students and colleagues? What stories can you recall that define exactly what experiences you do *not* want to create in your classroom?

Now try to remember the stories that your teachers told about *you*. Do you remember the letters of recommendation they wrote for you, highlighting your gifts, talents, and strengths? Do you remember times in which the adults told stories about you and your potential based on both your academic performance and your social interactions? Did familial patterns of behavior that older siblings displayed predetermine your expectations and possibilities? Did the adults tell stories about you that may or may not have accurately represented who you were not only as a student but also as a *person*?

As we prepare to let our story of Unstoppable Assessment unfold over the next several chapters, we encourage you to reflect on the kind of story that you are creating for, and about, your students. This collaborative team story is the essence of a professional learning community (PLC). Richard DuFour, Rebecca DuFour, Robert Eaker, Thomas W. Many, and Mike Mattos (2016) state that a PLC is an "ongoing process in which educators work collaboratively in recurring cycles of collective inquiry and action research to achieve better results for the students they serve" (p. 10). The questions you ask and the subsequent discussions that you hold as you reflect or as you work in teams will often closely align with the four critical questions that drive the work of a PLC (DuFour et al., 2016, p. 36):

1. What knowledge, skills, and dispositions should every student acquire as a result of this unit, this course, or this grade level?

2. How will we know when each student has acquired the essential knowledge and skills?

3. How will we respond when some students do not learn?

4. How will we extend the learning for students who are already proficient?

The team stories we offer throughout this book are real stories based on real teams and educators we know or have worked with. To maintain confidentiality, however, we choose not to identify individual educators' names or the schools or districts in which they work. Know that the examples we provide come from real practitioners approaching the work of collaborative teams together. To achieve maximum benefit, we highly recommend that as you use this resource and tools it contains, you do so within the context of a PLC or other collaborative team structure.

Educators in the 21st century have the power of the pen more than ever. We can take more responsibility for crafting a script, from beginning to end, that outlines the passion, hope, inspiration, and mobilization of effort we employ to focus on developing each student's academic readiness and disposition of character. Educators must be key authors in the language they use, the sequence of events they execute, and the climatic moments they aspire to in their critical work for students and for each other. One of the best ways to successfully accomplish this is through systems thinking.

Systems Thinking and Unstoppable Assessment

Douglas Fisher and Nancy Frey (2015), authors of *Unstoppable Learning: Seven Essential Elements to Unleash Student Potential*, outline systems thinking as *the* manner in which we, as teachers, approach the business of student learning. *Systems thinking* is the process of understanding how systems influence one another within a complete entity or larger system. Fisher and Frey (2015) drive home the importance of planning, launching, consolidating, assessing, adapting, managing, and leading learning in our classrooms in a *systemic* way. The authors assert, "Piecemeal approaches to improving teaching and learning are less than effective and often exhausting" (Fisher & Frey, 2015, p. 1). We'll take that advice to heart as we examine the assessment element of Unstoppable Learning (which we refer to as *Unstoppable Assessment*) in this book and offer a practical framework to deepen your assessment literacy and fluency.

Educators often find themselves in systems that are not as effective and efficient as they could be—systems that have yet to determine how all elements of the learning organization can work in harmony, systems where teachers and principals independently take care of business as they face situations in which they must ask, "If not me, then who?" We should leave very little about our work to a single individual to address, resolve, or create when such a significant matter—the achievement, growth, and development of our students—is at stake.

All too often, educators have the best-laid plans, and then the students show up! Something goes awry, and all of a sudden, it exposes a vulnerability in the system. It's often difficult to remedy that vulnerability in the moment. Systems thinking provides an avenue to proactively deal with vulnerability by understanding the interconnectedness among all the factors in the teaching and learning equation. The connections among all the *stuff* teachers need to do in preparation for students become more evident when we consider the patterns of thought and behavior that effective systems thinkers display, and their engagement with the four principles that are the basis for systems thinking.

Four Principles of Systems Thinking

Systems thinking requires educators to consider so much more than the task to complete or the steps in the process. Fisher and Frey (2015) define four harmonious principles for educators to consider as they strengthen learning systems for their students: (1) relationships, (2) communication, (3) responsiveness, and (4) sustainability. We suggest that the component of trust marries all four of these systems design principles together. Each of these principles will be threaded throughout the book's content and the conversations it elicits. Through our work across the globe, we have found many educators who employ these very principles yet continue to feel stifled and defeated in their efforts to design learning systems that support each student's growth and development. They feel either isolated as individuals or isolated as a team within their school, in their systems design work.

These educators are forward thinkers in a system that isn't designed to support them. We know that if we want to change our results, we have to change how we operate. For many schools, this means aligning in unity around a single focus of *learning* instead of perpetuating the cycles of organizational chaos that cause forward thinkers to become overwhelmed and debilitated in their work.

We believe the path to achieving this in assessment is by pairing the principles of systems thinking with the four elements of the Unstoppable Assessment framework: (1) seeking, (2) gathering, (3) discussing, and (4) responding to evidence. Table I.1 illustrates the four principles of systems thinking and their connections to our Unstoppable Assessment framework. It should be noted that the systems thinking principles aren't exclusive to individual elements of the Unstoppable Assessment framework. One specific principle does not align to one specific element. Rather, they work hand in hand to support assessment.

Table I.1: Principles of Systems Thinking for Unstoppable Assessment

Relationships	When students have the opportunity to invest in relationships with educators and other students present in their classrooms, they can more readily invest in their learning. Relationships in the classroom are not exclusively between two people, and each relationship can directly or indirectly affect each person in the learning environment.
Communication	The manner in which teachers communicate to, with, and about students, as people and as learners, can enhance—or disrupt—the climate and culture of the classroom community. As teachers discuss students and their learning pathways, teachers do so as though the students are in the room with them. Communication should advance learning and foster a lifelong commitment to doing so.
Responsiveness	Each student needs something unique throughout the learning process. The process must ensure that all learners have access to the necessary academic supports to get them from where they begin to where they need to go in order to perform at the expected level of mastery. Teachers should be responsive to the dynamic changes—both social-emotional and academic—that can occur from moment to moment within the classroom environment.
Sustainability	Differing expectations among teachers will yield differing success levels in learners. Teachers collaboratively work to determine a consistent level of performance—both academic and social—that is expected in all aspects of the learner's experience at school. Misalignment of student expectations will breed complacency and distract from the focus on learning for mastery for each student. Consistency, clarity, and cohesion create sustainable assessment practices and systems that each learner can readily understand.

We have linked the principles of systems thinking with our Unstoppable Assessment work in order to best prepare all educators for the thinking work that is necessary as they seek, gather, discuss, and respond to the student evidence from formative and summative assessments. The chapters in this book are respectively dedicated to each of these elements of the framework, which educators should exercise as they apply systems thinking to their considerations of student evidence and assessment.

About This Book

Chapter 1 lays the foundation for the first principle of systems thinking: relationships. We will focus on fostering trust through healthy relationships and honest communication among the adults within the learning organization. Chapters 2–5 guide you through the process of leveraging evidence-based assessment practices to build an aligned system of Unstoppable Assessment: seeking (chapter 2), gathering (chapter 3), discussing (chapter 4), and responding to evidence (chapter 5), respectively. Chapter 6 outlines important evidence-based practices that both teams and leaders can use to advance their work. This chapter focuses on leaders and teams using such practices to ensure sustainability when embedding elements of the systems thinking approach that are required for enacting an assessment plan.

The beginning of each chapter will ask you to consider three different perspectives, with suggested guiding questions around each perspective, that are associated with yielding high levels of student achievement.

1. **Zoom in:** These questions ask you to evaluate your team's current reality and assess what kind of information you need to move forward toward your goals.

2. **Zoom out:** These questions ask you to consider why you need the information presented and how it will advance your work.

3. **Panoramic:** These questions ask you to reflect on how the decisions you make or the conversations you have regarding the content will impact your system and what potential they have to create greater balance and alignment in your building or organization.

You will also encounter these types of questions in the reproducibles we offer throughout this book. These questions are meant to help guide discussion or reflection and, depending on the focus of each specific reproducible, may differ from the questions appearing at the beginning of the chapter. Visit **go.SolutionTree.com /assessment** to download the free reproducibles in this book.

 We have interspersed what we call *ponder boxes*, indicated with the symbol to the left, throughout the book to encourage readers to think deeply about the content and form their own conclusions and next steps. We encourage you to write notes or sketch drawings of your thoughts and reflections when you encounter these boxes.

Ponder Box

Consider the descriptors for each of the principles listed in table I.1 (page 4). Where are your points of pride? For which of these principles do you have opportunities for improvement? Jot down your initial thoughts in relation to your current practice of these principles of systems thinking.

We recognize that team discussions around each chapter may result in a variety of personal reflections and reactions—affirmations of some practices you and your team have already embedded into your assessment work, aha connections to tweak a practice or two within your system to further enhance what it can do for students, new laundry lists of questions, or an overwhelming sense of confusion on where to go next. No matter where you are on your journey, you are *exactly where you need to be* in order to take that next step forward. We have designed this book for all audiences, regardless of grade level, curricular area, or role in education. At the end of each chapter, we encourage you to complete reflection or planning activities before you and your teammates read the next chapter. These collaborative learning tasks are designed to inspire reflective thinking so you can more readily access each new piece of content while also fostering rich, productive dialogue within your team.

Before beginning chapter 1, take a moment to reflect on the collaborative nature of your learning organization. Check the boxes in the appropriate column in figure I.1 that represent your current approaches to learning.

Tasks I Approach in Isolation	Tasks I Approach Through Collaboration
☐ Reviewing standards I teach	☐ Reviewing standards I teach
☐ Clarifying learning targets	☐ Clarifying learning targets
☐ Designing scope and sequence or pacing	☐ Designing scope and sequence or pacing
☐ Developing lessons	☐ Developing lessons
☐ Writing common assessments	☐ Writing common assessments
☐ Determining scoring criteria for student mastery	☐ Determining scoring criteria for student mastery
☐ Reviewing students' work	☐ Reviewing students' work
☐ Determining next steps in instruction	☐ Determining next steps in instruction

Figure I.1: Approaches to learning.

*Visit **go.SolutionTree.com/assessment** for a free reproducible version of this figure.*

Ponder Box

Jot down or draw your reflection on your current state of isolated or collaborative learning based on your selections in figure I.1. What is the history behind your current reality? How will an awareness of that history help shape your future approaches to learning?

We know that pieces of the current reality you identified are within your control and other pieces are outside your realm. All these pieces matter, however, as we consider the development of sound assessment practices in our schools.

CHAPTER 1

BUILDING TRUST AND HEALTHY RELATIONSHIPS TO LEVERAGE ASSESSMENT

What we talk about is less important than how we talk about it and why we talk about it.

—Angela Freese

I t is the beginning of the first quarter at Kennedy Elementary School, and Emily is the veteran on her grade-level team, starting her third year of teaching second grade but her fifth year at Kennedy. Emily is well loved by her students and their families, and she has a true passion for teaching and learning. Her principal has begun to elevate her into leadership roles in the building, and she has recently been appointed chair of the building leadership team. Her energy is infectious, and she is a workhorse. She has the kind of stamina that a marathoner would envy.

Because of some retirements and transfers over the summer, Emily gets a brand-new set of teammates to begin this school year. Her three new colleagues are not new to teaching and bring a variety of experiences. Scott has moved from a neighboring district and has taught for seven years. Jordan has spent the last several years at home raising her children and is eager to get back into a school setting. Susan has just completed her master's degree and transferred from a fifth-grade teaching position at another school in the district to a second-grade position at Kennedy. Everyone clicks from the beginning, and the team takes opportunities to get to know each other personally as well. The team members agree that this is shaping up to be one of their best years of teaching—simply because they have each other!

At the end of the first quarter, Emily feels as though she and her teammates are cruising along in their first year together. However, as the team prepares for its weekly collaborative team meeting one morning, there is an unfamiliar emotional dynamic in the room. The team has just given an end-of-quarter common assessment in mathematics. The team members worked together to design the assessment—choosing standards, writing the questions, setting the scoring criteria, and agreeing on what mastery would look like. They created a Google sheet to organize all their student data in one place so that they can discuss the data together. They looked forward to celebrating their work and seeing where they can improve as a team. The meeting agenda is set to review the data, highlight patterns and trends, and plan next steps for corrective instruction and enrichment.

Up to this point, the team's meeting agendas helped lay the foundation for the team to function well together. The team members spent time developing their team norms and commitments, studied their state standards and reviewed the skills and concepts needed for students to show proficiency, developed lessons to teach those standards, and discussed instructional strategies they enjoy using with their students. They have not yet had an opportunity to review student work samples or analyze any collective data.

As the first-quarter team leader, Emily begins the meeting by reviewing the team's collective commitments and then dives into the agenda. "Thanks to everyone for entering your data into our shared spreadsheet," Emily begins. "Now we can see how all our students performed by class and as a whole grade level. We can really start to make meaning of how our teaching is impacting student learning!"

Jordan feels anxious about the meeting. She is skeptical of the process, and her data do not show the proficiency levels she hoped for. "I'm not so sure about this, Emily. I mean, why do we have to look at all our students together? Why can't we just examine our own class data and make adjustments based on what our individual results show?"

"I know it feels strange the first time, Jordan," says Scott. "We did something similar in my former district. Talking about our students as a whole helps us see our areas of strength as well as think about our next steps. Remember, one of our team norms is that we accept collective responsibility for each of our students. Working together as a team will make each of us stronger in our practice so that each of our students can become stronger."

Jordan still isn't convinced that this is the right plan for the team. With her data exposed, she feels as though people will pass judgment on her skill set as a teacher.

Susan, who has stayed quiet thus far, speaks up and echoes Jordan's concerns. "I agree with Jordan. I just don't understand why we have to put all our data out for everyone to see. Some of us did better than others. Emily, this whole data review thing was your idea, and your students got the best scores of any of us. Why did you really want us to share our data and compare us to each other?"

Emily sits in silence. She can't figure out what has gone wrong. Here she is, with her teammates who have become both colleagues and friends, and they are divided. Emily realizes that, although they have strong congenial relationships, they have not prepared themselves for the collaborative opportunity that this data conversation presents. In the face of this dissonance, Emily wonders, "Where do we go from here?"

Ponder Box

Have you ever felt like Emily in this team's story—you've designed great structures and been intentional in your planning, but all of a sudden, everything derails? Or have you felt like Jordan— vulnerable and exposed and fearful of what people might think about you and your teaching? How did you respond in these situations? What impact did your response have on your team? What next step should this team take?

This chapter will examine the importance of connecting all members of a school community so they produce the kind of effort that is needed to help all students succeed. As Fisher and Frey (2015) point out, "None of the relationships in the classroom is wholly separate from another" (p. 3). In this chapter, we examine relationships and the following aspects of building a collaborative culture: building the foundation of trust, defining collaboration, establishing norms and guidelines, valuing collective analysis, moving from positional hierarchy to collective commitment, and fostering healthy professional relationships.

- **Zoom in:** How do my behaviors and words show others that I am worthy of their trust?

- **Zoom out:** What strategies can we utilize to build trust among our colleagues? How will we intentionally plan opportunities within our organization to grow connections and develop relationships among members of teams?

- **Panoramic:** How might we seek, gather, discuss, and respond to evidence from our stakeholders that we are building trust and that positive adult relationships are strengthening the intended outcomes of our work as an organization?

Building the Foundation of Trust

Trust is the key when we ask educators to take risks, alter longstanding practices, and respond to assessment data in ways previously unseen. In cases where trust is lost, we see educators resort to doing their best in their own classrooms, and we get pockets of excellence instead of schools or districts of excellence. Educators spend their energy on self-protection and overcompliance—especially with those who have the power to discipline them—and this takes energy away from the collective purpose of the school.

Stephen Covey (2006) addresses the myths about trust in *The Speed of Trust: The One Thing That Changes Everything*. Table 1.1 provides a summary of these myths and the corresponding realities.

Table 1.1: Myths About Trust Versus Corresponding Realities

Myth	Reality
Trust is soft.	Trust is hard, real, and quantifiable.
Trust is slow.	Nothing is as fast as the speed of trust.
Trust is built solely on integrity.	Trust is a function of character (which includes integrity) and competence.
Either you have trust or you don't.	Trust can be both created and destroyed.
Once lost, trust cannot be restored.	Though difficult, in most cases lost trust can be restored.
You can't teach trust.	Trust can be effectively taught and learned.
Trusting people is too risky.	Not trusting people is a greater risk.
Trust is established one person at a time.	Establishing trust with one establishes trust with many.

Source: Covey, 2006, p. 25.

Ponder Box

Reflect on table 1.1 by answering the following questions.

- How do we build trust among our colleagues?

- How do my behaviors and words show others that I am worthy of their trust?

Trust influences student achievement. It is one of the factors that researchers Megan Tschannen-Moran and Wayne Hoy (2000) have found has greater impact than socioeconomic status as a predictor of future student achievement. Tschannen-Moran and Hoy (2000) state, "Trust is one party's willingness to be vulnerable to another party based on the confidence that the latter party is benevolent, reliable, competent, honest, and open" (p. 556). Let's look at each of these five facets: (1) benevolence, (2) reliability, (3) competency, (4) honesty, and (5) openness.

Benevolence

Hoy and Tschannen-Moran (2003) describe *benevolence* as the "confidence that one's well-being will be protected by the trusted party" (p. 186). In other words, as educators look to add to their successful practice while addressing the needs of a current group of students, does the leader exhibit the caring and compassion required when a difference of opinion on a staff occurs? When schools operate on the notion of presuming positive intention, team members embrace every struggle as an opportunity to provide more information and to bring colleagues along. Rather than condemning a person for asking a question or assuming he or she opposes the work, the team directs its effort at embracing another perspective on the challenges it collectively faces.

Reliability

Reliability is "the extent to which one can count on another person or group" (Hoy & Tschannen-Moran, 2003, p. 186). If colleagues feel they can work with each other through the highs and lows of their profession, and if individuals feel support when at their lowest ebb, then a team has established trust. If, instead, individuals feel as if everyone wants to vote them off the island, they become more reticent about engaging in a trusted relationship and pull back on any authentic engagement. They might simply defer to the team leader and become compliant.

Competency

Faith in the work ahead begins with faith in the person asking educators to embrace the work. If an individual does not possess the requisite skill to adopt a new practice, whom can he or she turn to? It could be the team or school leader, and it depends on his or her *competency*, or "the extent to which the trusted party has knowledge and skill" (Hoy & Tschannen-Moran, 2003, p. 186). If the work is also born of the collective commitment a team establishes, it feels much less as if it's being done *to* educators and more as if it's being done *by* educators and *for* educators. When leaders view their role as enabling educators, everyone owns the work collectively, leading to greater competency for all involved. This is in stark contrast to models that expect blind faith and compliance from educators.

Honesty

Nothing can replace honesty. Honesty does not mean always agreeing and being a ray of sunshine in every situation. It does mean having a willingness to confront realities and to share those openly and honestly with all team members—not just those among whom a strong connection might exist. Hoy and Tschannen-Moran (2003) describe *honesty* as "the character, integrity, and authenticity of the trusted party" (p. 186). In order to be trusted, the leader must be trustworthy.

Openness

Following honesty, openness implies equal treatment of all members of the team. We stress to teachers that they must build positive, caring relationships with every one of their students, even those who challenge them the most. We equally stress to leaders they must build positive, caring relationships with all teachers, even those who challenge them the most. Honesty is a complementary component to openness, which is driven by "the extent to which there is no withholding of information from others" (Hoy & Tschannen-Moran, 2003, p. 186).

The absence of any of these facets has the ability to derail progress and take away from building the trust necessary for great teams to function. If the only commonality a group of educators share is the school parking lot, the chances of true progress on the issue of assessment occurring will remain fleeting. This is hard work; it is messy work. It requires letting go of some things and embracing other things. All of this is possible with a collaborative team.

Defining Collaboration

The power of collaboration will not be a foreign concept to readers of this book. It simply makes sense that the power of *we* is superior to the power of *me*. As DuFour et al. (2016) write, "It is difficult to overstate the importance of collaborative teams in the improvement process" (p. 12). Despite that notion, collaboration is not always evident in every school or district. Ken Williams and Tom Hierck (2015) note this struggle when describing the dialogue that has occurred in some faculty meetings:

> Heated debates arose on whether collaboration really was possible and a desirable way to achieve the stated goals of a school. Detractors vehemently defended the practice of teaching in isolation—not because of any research that supports it, but because it is easier than collaboration. It's true: working together is a lot more challenging than working alone. Focusing on what we as teachers *can do* instead of on what we *don't have* requires a collective commitment. (p. 1)

Collaborative teams use data to reflect on teaching practices, monitor progress, and celebrate successes. They share the progress and the pitfalls and lean on each other to manage both. In a deeply intentional collaborative approach, everything is up for discussion as educators work to find ways to ensure all students attain the desired proficiency—not through lowering the bar but through elevating their teaching. This is not always easy and requires a high level of trust. As Fisher and Frey (2015) note, "The conversations in collaborative team meetings can scrape up against one's sense of self-efficacy, especially when presenting evidence about a lesson that failed to result in student learning" (p. 164). The absence of collaboration simply means educators don't have to confront such challenges with anyone but themselves, which often leads them to believe that the solution to these challenges lies in their students (or their students' parents or the system) needing to change.

Although collaboration is difficult, educators need to have collaborative conversations regarding assessment as they shift to what Tom Schimmer (2016) describes as "realigning the teaching and reporting processes to create a natural flow between assessments used to advance learning and assessments used to report it" (p. 18). They need to focus on collaborating to *add* to the teaching toolbox rather than to replace one tool with another. In order to manage these conversations, teams must establish norms and structures that drive how educators communicate.

Establishing Norms and Guidelines

A school team that functions effectively and supports high levels of learning for *all* students traces its success to the norms established through collective accountability. Effective teams *must* hold each other accountable to their norms in order to find success. Team norms are worthless if a team only writes them on paper and the entire team does not adhere to them. On teams composed of systems thinking educators, if someone arrives late to a meeting, doesn't honor the focus on student growth and success, or breaks any team norm, the rest of the team is willing to address that action by referring back to the agreed-on norms and ensuring that they are still desirable and will be followed. This responsibility can't fall to an external person (for example, the principal); it is something the group must manage. This action reflects the necessary collective accountability. Healthy teams effectively employ both gentleness and respect in their approach in order to promote the change in behavior they seek. Norms help the team define its levels of tolerance and how it will approach moments when those levels may be compromised. The end results for such teams are higher levels of learning, healthier team interactions, and strengthened relationships.

The purpose behind having a set of norms for a group to follow is to encourage behaviors that help the group do its work and discourage behaviors that interfere with a group's productivity. We can think of norms as the unwritten rules for how educators will act and what they will do. These rules govern how educators interact with each other, how they conduct the business of meetings, how they make decisions, and how they communicate these decisions. Here's the reality—whether or not educators take the time to establish norms, they are a part of every school's culture. These norms exist whether or not you acknowledge them or formalize them, and they may run contrary to any desired outcomes, as we will illustrate in the scenario later in this section.

It is also critical that each group of educators (based on department, grade level, role, and so on) creates its own set of *guidelines*. The guidelines are practical applications of the norms (behaviors), and the group must also discuss and develop these. If team members do not generate such guidelines, the behaviors described in the imposed norms may not align with what actually occurs. For example, a set of norms imposed on a team may include a guideline such as, "Electronic devices may be present during the meeting but only for the purposes of note taking." This guideline may quickly deflate the team's ability to most effectively and efficiently collaborate, as the team has much of its collective work shared among the team members via Google Docs (https://docs.google.com) and Google Sheets (www .google.com/sheets).

As such, each team member must take part in the norm development process to ensure that the norms align with the team's ability to do its best work. Furthermore, if team members feel unhappy with the norms they have received, violations may result in members feeling disgruntled with the idea of team norms rather than simply the display of unproductive adult behaviors. When healthy teams create their own norms, they can more swiftly and readily name violations. If a team does not create its own norms, however, then it will establish a de facto second (or third) set of norms. For example, a common norm is expecting everyone to arrive on time. If the team does not address violations, or only addresses them for some members, the message is clear—arriving on time is just a hope, not a norm. The team passively develops a second set of unspoken norms implying that they do not actually enforce the norms equally for everyone: *we say one thing, but we all know we actually do another.*

When teams create norms together and agree to hold each other accountable, the true challenge lies in ensuring that all team members actually implement and realize these intentions. Imagine this scenario: a group of teachers from across a district have an opportunity to meet for four full days over the course of the school year to develop common assessments for elementary literacy for their respective grade level. These meetings are a grind (usually six or seven hours of learning and development), but they are productive. One of the team members, however, uses each day as an opportunity to make a "softer" entry into the workday. She has decided that, because she has to *just* go to an all-day meeting—rather than get her classroom ready for students—she can wait at home a little longer to have another cup of coffee while she watches the morning news. She drops off some dry cleaning, stops at the post office, and then arrives at the meeting—a full hour after the meeting has begun. She also comes back late from the lunch break because of more personal errands.

At the end of the day, the team members comment, "Looks like it's going to be more of the same this year," regarding their teammate's punctuality.

A new team member asks why no one addresses this behavior with the late-arriving colleague. The other members say they addressed it in the past but the behavior didn't change.

At the next meeting, the same team member again arrives late by almost an hour. Over lunch, the new team member pulls her colleague to the side. She reminds her colleague that the team really values her input and her years of experience. The team members need her at the table for each minute of their collaboration so that they can build their collective expertise and get all the ideas in the room. The new team member then advocates her personal desire to have this colleague present to share her experiences and knowledge so that she can better develop her own capacity to contribute, being new to the team.

A few weeks later, at the third meeting, the chronically late team member arrives fifteen minutes early and brings a number of resources to share. She actively contributes to the conversation and helps grow her team's thinking so it can generate and develop the best ideas and plan for implementation. These new behaviors from this colleague are a notable difference from her past contributions to the team. Calling out team members doesn't have to sound like punishment. Rather, when colleagues take care of each other and put value in each other's presence, it allows each member to take ownership and make a commitment to the team as a whole.

There is something very unifying about our ability to align our collective energies and passions about our work and cohesively bring them together to develop shared expertise among the team. According to Jon Katzenbach and Douglas Smith (1993):

> The essence of a team is common commitment. Without it, groups perform as individuals; with it, they become a powerful unit of collective performance. . . . Teams develop direction, momentum, and commitment by working to shape a meaningful purpose. (p. 112)

Yet most teams need some ideas or protocols to frame their conversations and communications with each other to aid in the development of their thinking and planning. Once team members establish norms, they also may need some protocols to engage in advocacy and inquiry as a team. An example of how this engagement could unfold at a team meeting would be that teammates would exhibit *advocacy* by supporting colleagues in employing differentiation practices and would demonstrate *inquiry* when discussing whether the chosen instructional strategy worked or should be modified. DuFour, DuFour, Eaker, and Many (2010) outline some examples in tables 1.2 and 1.3 (pages 17–18).

Table 1.2: Protocols for Effective Advocacy

Protocol	Example
1. State your assumptions.	Here is what I think.
2. Describe your reasoning.	Here are some reasons why I arrived at this conclusion.

continued →

Protocol	Example
3. Give concrete examples.	Let me explain how I saw this work in another school.
4. Reveal your perspective.	I acknowledge that I am looking at this from the perspective of a veteran teacher.
5. Anticipate other perspectives.	Some teachers are likely to question . . .
6. Acknowledge areas of uncertainty.	Here is one issue you could help me think through.
7. Invite others to question your assumptions and conclusions.	What is your reaction to what I said? In what ways do you see things differently?

Source: DuFour et al., 2010, p. 135.

Table 1.3: Protocols for Effective Inquiry

Protocol	Example
1. Gently probe underlying logic.	What led you to that conclusion?
2. Use nonaggressive language.	Can you help me understand your thinking here?
3. Draw out their thinking.	Which aspects of what you have proposed do you feel are most significant or essential?
4. Check for understanding.	I'm hearing that your primary goal is . . .
5. Explain your reason for inquiring.	I'm asking about your assumption because I feel . . .

Source: DuFour et al., 2010, p. 135.

These protocols may assist teams in structuring the kinds of conversations that contribute to a school's positive momentum. They help both define and sustain the level of commitment needed to break through previous barriers.

Valuing Collective Analysis

When educators engage in collective analysis of student work as part of their assessment efforts, the benefit is that they establish the belief that this collective efficacy makes a difference for students. In essence, engaging in the work makes the work possible—a true self-fulfilling prophecy. As Nicole Dimich Vagle (2015) points out, "Collaborating with colleagues to tap into the expertise of the group can be a powerful means for finding innovative solutions that help all students learn at high levels" (p. 107). An equally important collateral benefit is that educators tap into others' brilliance and strengthen their teacher toolboxes.

Time is the most precious resource in schools. Educators know this, and in an effort not to waste time, teams sometimes reach decisions that lead to more individual work than teamwork. It seems logical to divide a task up and then report back to the larger group whenever they can wedge a meeting into the busy schedule. This rush to expediency, however, undermines any effort at collective analysis. Individuals become fluent in their part of the process but not in the whole initiative. Although initially more time-consuming, involving all educators in all aspects of the implementation of or shift in assessment practice produces a critical mass of people who completely own the work and are willing to push forward with the ongoing practice. Collective analysis does not depend on any one individual and can sustain the personnel changes that schools and districts routinely go through. If, instead, one or two key individuals (team or school leaders) own the bulk of the work and they leave to pursue other opportunities, the initiative may either end or begin to fragment. This approach may lead those still at the site to feel cynical toward the initiative and may inevitably doom the work. The notion of the flavor-of-the-month cycle that schools go through may drive a negative view of this crucial work.

Collective analysis connects to assessment work via the following five steps.

1. Record student data with agreed-on scoring guide levels (such as *exemplary*, *proficient*, *approaching*, and *below*), and display them on a data wall or in a data room.

2. Analyze data so that accurate and evidence-based inferences can be drawn, rather than opinion-based inferences.

3. Establish goals (such as strategic and specific, measurable, attainable, results-oriented, and time-bound [SMART] goals) that will drive the work of the unit and be monitored throughout, including at the end of the unit.

4. Determine which teaching strategies might work to meet the goals, and have alternate strategies at the ready for those situations (such as student struggles) that emerge and could not be reasonably anticipated.

5. Build a plan to guide next steps based on what emerges from the previous steps.

You must attune this work to the context of your school and your team, and you must also make it non-negotiable. Without collective analysis based on the needs of all students, the chances of moving the proficiency needle remain more of a hope than a goal. Larry Ainsworth and Donald Viegut (2006) suggest that teams that follow some process of collective data analysis will receive four key benefits:

1. Using the common formative pre-assessment results, teachers can plan differentiated instruction for individual students needing intervention or acceleration.

2. Using the common formative post-assessment results, teachers will gain meaningful and timely feedback on their instructional effectiveness. . . .

3. Comparing the results of the pre- and post-assessments, teachers will have credible evidence as to individual student improvement gains.

4. Collaborating with colleagues from different areas of specialization, teachers will contribute to and benefit from the collective wisdom of everyone involved. (p. 94)

As educators achieve more and more success with this collective analysis and see student learning results improve, it fosters a collective belief that the work is doable and *all* learners can succeed.

Moving From Positional Hierarchy to Collective Commitment

As school teams foster their collaborative practices and begin to describe their collective commitments, they must intentionally monitor the translation of those commitments into practice. Each conversation and each collaborative experience should represent the idea that *one voice* transparently communicates and models the commitments that teams have made. This can be easier said than done.

Positional hierarchy exists in every school or district regardless of size or location. Left unchecked, it will guide how all members of a school community are treated, based on their position within the school or district. This encourages compliance—often for fear of reprisal if dissent occurs—at each meeting, with very little progress. Collective commitment, on the other hand, engenders shared ownership and fosters a desire to work together on behalf of *our* students.

Trust and positive relationships are two of the outcomes of collective commitment. If schools and districts don't move from compliance to commitment, then the likelihood of improving learning for both students and educators will seem more like a wish than a reality. While it may be advantageous in the early start of any new initiative to have more compliance than commitment, the problem emerges when schools and districts remain trapped in a cycle of compliance without evolving toward commitment. In a cycle of compliance, educators eagerly take responsibility for the results of the already-proficient students ("look how well my top students did") while blaming either the owner of the initiative ("your plan for our school didn't work") or external factors (students' home life, familial support, poverty, and so on) that are beyond a school's control for the results of any low-achieving students. If unmonitored, positional hierarchy can absolve those not in a leadership role of any responsibility for improving the outcomes and can contribute to the creation of a toxic school culture where policies, procedures, and practices that defend and preserve the status quo are in place. We must foster healthy professional relationships if we are to prevent or interrupt positional hierarchy in our schools.

Fostering Healthy Professional Relationships

Anthony Bryk, Penny Bender Sebring, Elaine Allensworth, Stuart Luppescu, and John Easton (2010) conclude, "Relationships are the lifeblood of activity in a school community" (p. 137). Any one person going it alone will not accomplish the high-quality work that stakeholders expect in schools, regardless of his or her prodigious talent. Let's be clear; we are not saying you need to develop personal friendships with all the other adults in the school building. We are talking about having a healthy level of respect and trust in all the colleagues you work with based on their knowledge, experience, and desire to make a difference and serve students. You cannot rush this, and in situations where healthy professional relationships have not been the norm, barriers might exist that teams need to address. Bryk et al. (2010) suggest:

> In short, relational trust is forged in day-to-day social exchanges. Through their actions, school participants articulate their sense of obligation toward others, and others in turn come to discern the intentionality enacted here. Trust grows over time through exchanges in which the expectations held for others are validated by actions. (p. 139)

When we are purpose driven, all the policies, procedures, and actions any member of the school community engages in align with that purpose. Personal opinions dissipate, to be replaced with the collective commitment to *our* cause. The more individuals show they are worthy of trust (aligning actions to purpose), the more trusted they become. Healthy, positive relationships grow through our mutual commitment to our purpose as a learning organization.

Understanding the current status of the trust and relationships among educators is key—not as an attempt to create friction or to castigate any colleagues but to establish a baseline for future planning and growth opportunities and to build trust and foster healthy relationships. This also provides the opportunity to celebrate those areas that work exceedingly well as teams push forward. The survey in figure 1.1 (page 22) adapts surveys from DuFour et al. (2010) and Susan Stephenson (2009). It is designed to identify both strengths and growth opportunities for teams. Teams should place a check mark in the column that corresponds to their current reality for each statement.

Statement	Strongly Agree	Agree	Disagree	Strongly Disagree
My colleagues willingly share their materials, resources, and ideas with me.				
I believe my colleagues have good intentions in their interactions with me.				
I am not afraid to share student learning results with my colleagues.				
I believe that everyone on my team makes meaningful contributions.				
Our team celebrates our collective accomplishments.				
Staff work together effectively to achieve school goals.				
Input for decisions is valued from all staff members.				
I feel that others value my work and my contributions.				

Source: Adapted from DuFour et al., 2010; Stephenson, 2009.

Figure 1.1: Survey to evaluate your current reality.

*Visit **go.SolutionTree.com/assessment** for a free reproducible version of this figure.*

Concluding Thoughts to Heighten Systems Thinking

When you started reading this chapter, you may have thought, "I bought this book to learn more about assessment. Why do the authors spend the first chapter talking about building trust and growing healthy relationships?" We contend that if you weren't too sure about our methods before, you have a better understanding of them now. The truth of the matter is that the professional relationships we strive to cultivate as adults are exactly the same as the healthy relationships we strive to build with our students in our classrooms and school communities. We desire to create classroom cultures where students learn how to work collaboratively and communicate effectively, whether or not they like each other. We build team spirit and foster ways for students to benefit from common goals and victories. As teachers, we expect our students to communicate that message too. We know we cannot achieve community in our classrooms if the teacher is the only one cheering from the sidelines. Similarly, as adults, we cannot expect that our principal or district staff can carry the torch alone. Building trust starts with one conversation, and each ensuing conversation further develops it.

Before moving to the next chapter, please take a moment to evaluate your current reality using the survey in figure 1.1. Team members should fill out the survey independently and then come together to discuss their responses.

Ponder Box

Consider your reflections at the beginning of this chapter on table 1.1 (page 12). Do you have any additional reflections now that you've finished reading this chapter? Circle back to your initial thoughts, and grow them further by writing down any new ideas, strategies, or reflections that have come to light.

CHAPTER 2

SEEKING EVIDENCE TO LAUNCH ASSESSMENTS WITH THE END IN MIND

To begin with the end in mind means to start with a clear understanding of your destination. It means to know where you're going so that you better understand where you are now and so that the steps you take are always in the right direction.

—Stephen Covey

n *Results Now*, Mike Schmoker (2006) asserts that "the best explanation for why our schools aren't far more successful, intellectually engaging places is fairly simple: the most important people within and outside schools know very little about what actually goes on inside them" (p. 13). This gives us great pause. How can this be? Ask any teacher how his or her students perform in the classroom, and most can give you a synopsis of which students are at grade level, which students may be above grade level, and which students continue to demonstrate difficulty. After all, teachers have responsibility for the safety, well-being, and educational potential of each student. It only stands to reason that they would have the best idea of what level of learning is happening in each classroom.

If we took our question one step further and asked teachers *how* they have come to know this information, however, we might receive varied responses showing that different teachers use different criteria to reach their conclusions on students' performance. For example, one ninth-grade mathematics teacher might use grades or marks from end-of-unit or chapter tests to make that determination. Another may use a combination of assessments and work samples to draw that conclusion, utilizing rubrics and other common scoring criteria to determine what information students have learned. A third may use a balanced system of assessment—summative and formative, formal and informal—as well as classroom work samples, collaborative peer work, and feedback loops between the student and teacher to reasonably ascertain what his students know and what they can do with what he has taught them. As you can see, the three teachers use vastly different information to draw significant conclusions about the academic performance of each student. These educators run the risk of leaving a student's academic experience to chance when they make decisions independently from one another regarding what students are expected to learn—and therefore where the teachers will spend time teaching in their classrooms. Williams and Hierck (2015) further explain:

> They will send three groups of ninth-grade students to tenth grade who are prepared differently. And the tenth-grade mathematics teachers will then face students of varying strengths and levels of preparedness, and they will spend precious time filling gaps among all three groups of students before they can begin tenth-grade instruction. (p. 108)

With this variability comes the assurance that each student will have similar variability in his or her preparedness for the next level of learning. To avoid such discrepancies, teams must ensure consistency, clarity, and coherence around what learning they expect from students and how they will determine the evidence of that learning about what students know and can do. As Fisher and Frey (2015) remind us, "The keystone of effective assessment is the teacher's ability to articulate how students can demonstrate what they have mastered" (p. 90). This chapter outlines four foundational elements needed to ensure this consistency, clarity, and coherence: (1) a guaranteed and viable curriculum, (2) collaborative team structures and processes, (3) a common set of priority standards by course, and (4) a common scope and sequence. We illustrate how teams can intentionally establish these elements by beginning with the end in mind.

- **Zoom in:** What norms and commitments do we make to share ownership of the success of all students and work interdependently to achieve a goal? What kind of information do we need to ensure all students experience a learning environment that enables them to attain high levels of achievement?

- **Zoom out:** How will each teacher ensure that every student acquires the most essential knowledge and skills for that unit of study? How does our assessment design marry with our instructional framework to enable all students to achieve the desired results?

- **Panoramic:** What is the connection between creating a common scope and sequence across the team and building a guaranteed and viable curriculum for students?

Guaranteed and Viable Curriculum

In order to effectively seek (and then gather, discuss, and respond to) evidence of student learning, we must first have a systematically designed plan that carefully outlines what we expect students to learn and to what level they need to learn it. Fisher and Frey (2015) state, "Every teacher should deeply understand what evidence he or she expects as an indication of learning *before* the first lesson is ever delivered" (p. 103). Not only do we want every teacher to have an understanding of these learning expectations, but we want to set up every *team* to develop a common understanding. With that comes the expectation that each team, for each course or subject delivered, will determine—and then implement—the guaranteed and viable curriculum that students will learn. Collaborative team members across a district must understand that a *guaranteed and viable curriculum* (GVC) accomplishes two things: (1) gives students access to the same essential learning regardless of who teaches their class and (2) can be taught in the time allotted (Marzano, 2003). DuFour et al. (2016) further emphasize:

> It does not mean that teachers must adhere to lockstep pacing by which members are teaching from the same page on the same day. It does not mean that all teachers must use the same instructional strategies or same materials. It does mean that during a unit presented within a specific window of time established by the team . . . each team member will work to ensure every student acquires the knowledge and skills the team has agreed are most essential for that unit. (p. 113)

This message may evoke a different reaction from each individual teacher as well as across each grade-level or content-area team. It is normal to feel apprehensive about implementing new processes and procedures. In the following sections, we will discuss the importance of embracing the fears team members may feel about the change this involves and introduce a continuum to help teams assess and plan their trajectory for implementing changes toward ensuring a guaranteed and viable curriculum.

Embracing Our Fears

Despite our schooling, experience, professional development, and capability to rely on our team to work interdependently to achieve high levels of learning for every student, many educators remain fearful of the word *guaranteed* when it comes to curriculum and work with students. We hear this fear reflected in questions we've received in our professional work, such as, What if we have students come into our classrooms who struggle to read? What if some of our students are challenged with social and emotional needs that prevent them from actively engaging in the classroom? and What if I am the only teacher in my grade or content area and I don't have a team of teachers to rely on for support, guidance, or reflection?

We believe that a guarantee is exactly what educators need to overcome these fears. Strengthening learning systems in classrooms calls for more than a tweak of practice; it calls for a transformation. A collective commitment to honor this guarantee supports the obligation to provide the best for every student every day. A guarantee provides assurance that all students will receive access to the same rigorous content, no matter which teacher delivers the instruction. A guarantee instills confidence that we will adequately and intentionally prepare each student with the academic skills and dispositions of character needed for success in college and career. A guarantee inspires teachers and students alike to ensure mastery of the most essential content and leverage those skills across multiple disciplines to further deepen understanding and application during new learning. Given its potential to yield high levels of student growth and achievement, the word *guaranteed* could actually minimize fear and instead empower and invigorate the work.

In addition to being guaranteed, curriculum must also be viable for every student to attain. A GVC demonstrates value in what all students are expected to learn. The term *viable* ensures that teachers have enough time to deliver the guaranteed content and that students have enough opportunities to learn it. No matter which teacher works with their child, all parents get assurance that the level of academic rigor is consistent and their child will receive the time and space needed to master the essential skills and concepts. A GVC requires a teacher to stay committed to the agreed-on content, but it does not prescribe exactly how to teach it. This distinction allows for each teacher to let his or her individual gifts, talents, and passions around the content shine through and heighten the relevance and engagement for students. A GVC is tight on *what* students need to learn but is loose on *how* all teachers ensure that students will learn it.

Using a Continuum to Assess Current Realities

We have outlined a continuum to help teachers assess their place on their journey to making learning the foundational purpose of their work. The continuum is broken down into three topical areas (see figures 2.1–2.3, pages 30–35), based on the three factors we have identified that contribute to a GVC: (1) collaborative team structures and processes, (2) a common set of priority standards by course, and (3) a common scope and sequence by course. The four columns indicate four general stages along the continuum. We intentionally left the middle Strengthening and Mobilizing columns blank because we do not want teachers to get caught up in the minutiae of specific verbiage. We want teachers to collaboratively develop their next steps and determine which behaviors or actions will propel the team toward the Championing stage. Consider instead the ways in which your team can dialogue in relation to the Engaging side and the Championing side of the continuum. (Note: If you find yourself in a situation where you do not have *any* of these conversations with your team or school, please connect with your building principal or district leadership. Our continuum honors the decades of research cited throughout our text, and as such, we chose to start our continuum at the first next step *beyond* "Our team is not yet engaged in these conversations.")

Some teachers respond to a GVC via the Engaging stage; they have received copies of their standards or a curriculum guide, but they have no process to discuss curriculum with their colleagues or any expectation that they would do so. The absence of district direction has the potential to paralyze some well-intentioned, hardworking teams. Without systems that give teachers both the time and space to do the work and a guided process for what to discuss and how to work effectively, some of our best and brightest find few eager collaborators and end up finding greater solace in the autonomous nature of their individual classroom.

Some teachers are ready to place themselves in the Championing stage on the continuum. Their departments have already received the time and space to collaborate, and as such, the teachers have established the expected learning outcomes for their students. They share ownership for every student on the team and work tirelessly to make sure that each student gets the instructional supports needed for success. They know that any student can reach any target, so long as it stays clear and constant for him or her to work toward (Stiggins, Arter, Chappuis, & Chappuis, 2004). When teams gain clarity and coherence on what the essential learning is and hold consistent expectations for what student success will look like, every student can achieve success.

Many teachers, however, land somewhere between these two extremes. Some may have taken part in past district teams that formed to create curricular documents and guidelines, but those teams did not intentionally disseminate that work, and the system included no accountability for making sure that all teachers implemented the work that others created. Some teachers try to use these documents to pace their lessons appropriately and to gather solid, accurate information from students about what they are learning, but they lack instructional materials from the district or collaborative team supports from their colleagues to accomplish this meaningful work.

Unstoppable Assessment Connection to a GVC	Stages of the Continuum			
	Engaging	**Strengthening**	**Mobilizing**	**Championing**
	We are beginning to tackle this work as a team. We are creating commitments and making sense of how we will collaborate together for each other and for our students.	Our team is beginning to implement our discussions and apply what we are learning in our work together as a team.	Our team is collecting evidence on the effectiveness of our work and how students are impacted. We have consistency in practice and frequent dialogue about our work.	Our team has developed an aligned system of support for each other and for students. Students—their work, their growth, and their achievement—are the focus of our conversations. We are unstoppable as a team, and our students learn more because of our collaborative conversations.
Common Purpose	As a team, we identify what is important to us as individuals. Norms are identified by team members for further discussion.			Each team member represents his or her common purpose both in words and behaviors. This means we follow the norms and protocols we have established and we speak with one voice about our work as a team.
Team Meeting Systems	Discussion begins with where we can set aside time for our important collaborative dialogue. Roles for team members are discussed, and a framework for meetings is identified.			We have time during the school contractual day to meet, which supports both horizontal and vertical alignment across our building. We have set specific processes that support how our time is used and how to record our ideas and action plans to promote sustainability in our efforts.

Growth Mindset	Our work begins with a commitment to presume positive intention. Important dialogue is held on the meaning of collaboration, the identification of strengths and growth opportunities, and collective commitment.	We know that each team member's voice is valued, and we ensure each is heard in our work. Everyone contributes ideas, templates, or strategies to better the team as a whole. We rely on each other to ensure our students learn more. Our synergy enables us to be our collective best.
Celebration and Determination	We have made plans to identify early milestones and commit to celebrating growth as it is attained. Celebration is aligned with our collective commitment. Data are discussed as being the important evidence needed.	Our team meetings provide a safe environment to share and compare our student results so that we can learn from each other and develop best practices. We celebrate both our individual and collective achievements related to our goals. We are better because of each other.

Figure 2.1: Unstoppable Assessment connection to a GVC—Collaborative team structures and processes.

Unstoppable Assessment Connection to a GVC	Stages of the Continuum			
	Engaging	Strengthening	Mobilizing	Championing
	We are beginning to tackle this work as a team. We are creating commitments and making sense of how we will collaborate together for each other and for our students.	Our team is beginning to implement our discussions and apply what we are learning in our work together as a team.	Our team is collecting evidence on the effectiveness of our work and how students are impacted. We have consistency in practice and frequent dialogue about our work.	Our team has developed an aligned system of support for each other and for students. Students—their work, their growth, and their achievement—are the focus of our conversations. We are unstoppable as a team, and our students learn more because of our collaborative conversations.
Shared Knowledge of Standards	Standards are viewed in grades and across grades. The team begins to seek consensus on what the standards mean and what level of performance is needed for mastery. Methods of data tracking are delineated as the purpose for gathering this information.			We have collectively reviewed our state standards in order to understand what students should know and to what level they should know it. We regularly analyze our achievement data to look for patterns and trends to confirm we are teaching to the level required for student mastery or discover opportunities to improve our work.

Collective Agreement of Essential Content	Individuals cherry-pick which standards are priority, without common process or discussion. Vertical alignment is sought as a component of our work.	We have collectively used the criteria of endurance, leverage, and readiness—as well as tested highly for accountability and student-need driven—in order to determine which standards we will prioritize in our work. We regularly monitor this subset of standards and provide corrective instruction when students have not yet demonstrated the expected levels of mastery.
Student Investment	The power of student investment and engagement is discussed by our team. We plan strategies to increase the capacity of our students as partners in the learning experience. This includes intentional teaching of peer assessment and instruction.	All students understand what academic mastery looks like and sounds like in their classroom. Students work in partnership with their teachers to determine where they are as compared to where they need to be in their learning. Students are invested in their work because they clearly understand what the expectations are and how they will achieve those expectations.
Active Monitoring	We begin to discuss a plan for monitoring our work as well as options for departments and the staff to analyze evidence.	We have an intentional plan for monitoring the learning of our agreed-on priority standards. We use that information to guide our instructional planning for and response to students.

Figure 2.2: Unstoppable Assessment connection to a GVC—Common set of priority standards.

Unstoppable Assessment	Stages of the Continuum			
Connection to a GVC	Engaging	Strengthening	Mobilizing	Championing
	We are beginning to tackle this work as a team. We are creating commitments and making sense of how we will collaborate together for each other and for our students.	Our team is beginning to implement our discussions and apply what we are learning in our work together as a team.	Our team is collecting evidence on the effectiveness of our work and how students are impacted. We have consistency in practice and frequent dialogue about our work.	Our team has developed an aligned system of support for each other and for students. Students—their work, their growth, and their achievement—are the focus of our conversations. We are unstoppable as a team, and our students learn more because of our collaborative conversations.
Timeline for Instructional Delivery	We establish pacing calendars that look at when the priority learning can be achieved. All factors in a school year are examined for impact.			We agree and adhere to common windows of time when essential content will be taught and monitored and mastery will be acquired during the course of instruction. Each team member understands what we are doing and why we are doing it.

Balanced Assessment	We identify all assessments currently in place and their potential impact on student learning. Discussion of the impact on effective formative practice on the summative requirements is pursued.	We have designed a plan for monitoring student learning of the priority standards in a timely manner and have collaboratively developed common assessment tools. Our assessment plan includes team-developed formative assessments, coupled with preassessments, midunit checkpoints for understanding, and end-of-unit and end-of-grading-period assessments.
Instructional Agility	We believe assessment is necessary for planning optimal teaching strategies and learning experiences. The purpose of our assessments is aligned with discovering, not describing.	We use our data from our common assessments to guide differentiation—both intervention and enrichment—and pacing during each unit of study to interrupt student misconceptions in the moment and provide corrective instruction toward mastery.

Figure 2.3: Unstoppable Assessment connection to a GVC—Common scope and sequence.

Ponder Box

How might you describe your team's behaviors and practices regarding these Unstoppable Assessment connections to a guaranteed and viable curriculum? Where are you strong? Where might you have opportunities for development?

Utilizing a continuum offers each teacher the opportunity to recognize the work he or she has already done and provides a clear picture for attainment of success and sustainability moving forward. Teachers can see their next steps and begin to work through the process for attaining the next level collaboratively. The big idea here is that no matter which principal leads the building or which people serve at the district office, this continuum reflects the level of work that we expect among teachers in order to represent student learning as our primary purpose. The valuable takeaway is that a GVC is an essential component of a healthy instructional system, and it serves as a prerequisite to creating an Unstoppable Assessment system.

The marriage of assessment, curricular, and instructional practices via a GVC allows for the design of a system within classrooms that promotes mastery with high levels of engagement and collaboration among students and teachers. In the following sections, we will further clarify those three factors that contribute to a guaranteed and viable curriculum: (1) collaborative team structures and processes, (2) a common set of priority standards by course, and (3) a common scope and sequence by course.

Ponder Box

Consider the following question as a team: What kind of evidence do we need to ensure all students experience a learning environment that enables them to achieve high levels of learning?

Collaborative Team Structures and Processes

In our work with schools, we stress the importance of achieving a collective commitment through deep and meaningful collaborative efforts. This does not imply universal agreement on every topic every time. Instead, it suggests a high regard and respect for what every educator brings to the conversation. It creates trust that allows tough issues to surface, various perspectives to be shared, and an even better plan to be enacted that aligns with the desired goal of improving student outcomes. It's important that teams examine and clarify the following two conditions as they create the shared mission of their school.

1. *We* believe that all students can learn at high levels.

2. *We* make the commitment to ensure learning for every student.

These two statements tend to generate healthy dialogue around what the terms *high levels*, *ensure*, and *every* mean, which teams need to process as the root of their work toward establishing their mission and as the route to take regarding the steps of that work. Refer back to the discussion on collaboration and norms in chapter 1 as you work through your team's desired outcomes and recognize the effort you need to put forth to make these two conditions a reality in your school. As teams build collaborative structures and processes, they can begin by engaging the team in discussion around two key questions: (1) What norms and commitments will we make to share ownership of the success of all students and work interdependently to achieve a goal? and (2) How will we use student work sampling and data to identify and enhance instructional practices that work?

Ponder Box

Take a moment to jot down or draw your initial thoughts about collaborative team structures and processes based on the information in this section. You can refer back to these notes later in the chapter as you and your teammates begin to work through the next section of the conversation.

Common Set of Priority Standards by Course

Robert Marzano (2003) suggests that we have entirely too much content to teach our students in the time allotted for their preK–12 experience. We want to make it clear that the standards identified in state, provincial, or national legislation are important and have been deemed necessary for students to learn. Also, these standards require our students to exhibit certain dispositions (for example, collaboration and communication) in order to maximize their achievement of the standards' expectations. We simply assert that we cannot treat all standards equally. Certain standards hold greater weight—or significance—than others and may require more time, a larger allotment of resources, or more specificity in order to ensure that all students have appropriately mastered them. As such, the collective work of educators yields the highest levels of achievement for students when we collaboratively work to unpack (unwrap, deconstruct, and analyze) and then prioritize standards to identify the most essential learning. When building a common set of priority standards, teams can prepare their mindset using these two questions: (1) What is this standard asking of our students? and (2) What level of impact does the acquisition of this knowledge have on our students?

Experts and thought leaders on this subject have already created various templates, protocols, and processes to support teachers as they begin this prioritizing conversation (Ainsworth, 2003; Bailey, Jakicic, & Spiller, 2014; Erkens, 2016; Wiggins & McTighe, 2005). We have provided you with another example of a tool that supports this conversation later in this chapter (see the Priority Standards and Assessment Plan Template, figure 2.5, page 40). Getting started can be the trickiest part. As educators reflect on their instructional and assessment practices, they might realize that sometimes it's hard enough for them to agree on which targets are the *right* ones to measure, let alone for teams to agree on what success looks like and sounds like for the targets measured! At the beginning of these collaborative conversations, educators have three initial questions to consider: (1) What are the most essential learning targets to highly monitor? (2) Why do we believe these to be most essential? and (3) How can we intentionally plan our instruction to ensure that we give students enough opportunities to learn what we expect to the level we expect it? Answering these questions moves teams closer to achieving the primary purpose of high levels of learning for every student. The remainder of this section describes one team's process as it engaged in these conversations and approached this work.

The team began by cutting its standards document into strips so that each standard was independent from the others. The team then taped each strip to the wall and evaluated each standard based on the following five criteria, adapted from Douglas Reeves (2002) and Larry Ainsworth (2003).

1. **Endurance:** Will the standard provide students with knowledge and skills that will have value beyond a single test date?

2. **Leverage:** Will the standard provide knowledge and skills that will have value in multiple disciplines?

3. **Readiness for the next level of learning:** Will the standard provide students with the essential knowledge and skills necessary for success in the next grade or the next level of instruction?

4. **Accountability:** Will an accountability feature (state, provincial, or national test or district benchmark) test the standard?

5. **Student needs:** What do our data suggest students need relative to their academic, social, or emotional learner attributes for mastery?

The team used the template in figure 2.4 to identify its standards and check how these five areas align with the standard to determine which standards are priorities.

Directions: Enter each standard in the far-left column. For each of the five criteria, document whether the standard meets that specific criterion. Then, provide your reasoning or evidence regarding the decision your team made. Once you document each standard, review the evidence to determine which standards your team will prioritize. Remember, a standard may not meet all the criteria for the team to agree it should be prioritized.

Subject area: _____ Date: _____

Standard	Endurance		Leverage		Readiness		Accountability		Student Needs	
	Yes or No	Why or How?	Yes or No	Why or How?	Yes or No	Why or How?	Yes or No	Why or How?	Yes or No	Why or How?

Ready for the next step? Talk with your vertical teams, and check for alignment across grade levels and content areas.

Figure 2.4: Consensus-building tool for prioritizing standards.

Visit go.SolutionTree.com/assessment for a free reproducible version of this figure.

As you can imagine, some very passionate dialogue ensued. The team referred to some standards as *low-hanging fruit*—easy to pick off and reach consensus that they met the criteria for the most essential learning. Other standards were less obvious. Disagreement arose over whether certain whole standards were essential or just certain elements within the standards. In these situations, the teachers considered another question: What would students need to do in order to show mastery of this standard? Determining how students would actually need to demonstrate their knowledge and application of the content they were taught enabled the team to think strategically and intentionally and to repurpose the dialogue back to the initial criteria.

Through the organic nature of the dialogue, Angie guided the team to design a template, as illustrated in figure 2.5, to help focus the team's conversations and guide the thinking around prioritizing standards.

Priority Standard	Learning Targets *I can* statements	Methods of Assessment How will students show what they know?	Pacing and Instructional Considerations Where does this appear in my curriculum?

Figure 2.5: Priority standards and assessment plan template.

The team added its newly identified priority standards to the template and, from there, began to tease out specific learning targets that would better describe what students should know and be able to do in order to demonstrate mastery on each of those standards (Vagle, 2015). *Learning targets* are the most discrete pieces of information embedded in the language of a standard that teachers can assess to determine a student's collective understanding of the standard as a whole (Erkens, 2016). These learning targets enable both the teacher and the student to more clearly identify the necessary pathway to perform at the level of rigor that the standard requires. Identifying these learning targets is pivotal for clarifying what student success will look like and sound like as a team intentionally plans its instruction.

Next, the team evaluated the specific language of each standard and the corresponding learning targets to "make the match" between the rigor of the learning targets and the appropriate assessment methods by which to gather evidence from students. This evidence serves as high-yield feedback between the student and teacher in regard to student progress toward mastery of the learning targets.

And finally, the team reflected on its current scope and sequence to identify moments in the curriculum pacing where these priority standards came to life. As the team members implemented their curriculum, they could consider whether their curriculum pacing adequately prepared students to achieve the level of mastery required by the end of the year. This process encouraged them to reflect on their current instructional practices while also reflecting forward to ensure that they give students enough learning activities to best prepare them to meet the level of rigor required in order to successfully demonstrate mastery.

Figure 2.6 (pages 42–43) is an example of this team's initial work. The team derived and adapted its priority standards from the Common Core State Standards for English language arts (National Governors Association for Best Practices [NGA] & Council of Chief State School Officers [CCSSO], 2010). The example in figure 2.6 serves as evidence of this team's very first conversation around this work, which the team members will most certainly revisit and revise based on their experiences. However, we include this example here because it honors the way in which systems thinking teams work toward continuous improvement, in that our first thoughts often may not be our last thoughts. Our collaborative team conversations enable us to regularly revisit our decisions and use evidence from our practices to determine whether we want to continue implementing those decisions in the future. For example, this team initially began defining their pacing and instructional considerations relative to specific novels. Past practice for this team had been to adopt specific novels to use with the entire class to teach the identified literacy standards. However, as this book goes to publication, this team is revisiting how they pace and plan in order to more proactively address students' needs and ensure that the text sets they use promote both instructional and independent levels of reading for students. Additionally, this team has begun collaboratively developing rubrics to align with their learning targets. Students can visualize what the performance expectations are and gain greater clarity on how their work represents evidence of learning in alignment with those performance expectations. Embedding continuous improvement and reflection as a consistent part of our educational practice adds great value.

Priority Standard	Learning Targets *I can* statements	Methods of Assessment How will students show what they know?	Pacing and Instructional Considerations Where does this appear in my curriculum?
Write clear and coherent texts in which the development, organization, and style are appropriate to task, purpose, and audience.	• I can clearly express my ideas in written language. • I can organize my ideas in written form according to the task.	• Character analysis • Theme analysis • Claim, Support, Explain (at least one formative per unit) • Claim, Support, Explain (one summative per semester)	• *To Kill a Mockingbird* or *Of Mice and Men* • *A Long Way Gone* • Each unit and novel • *Animal Farm* or *To Kill a Mockingbird* and *Romeo and Juliet*
Write arguments to support claims in analysis of substantive topics or texts, using valid reasoning and relevant and sufficient evidence.	• I can support my claim with logical reasoning. • I can support my claim with specific textual evidence.	• Character analysis • Theme analysis • Claim, Support, Explain (at least one formative per unit) • Claim, Support, Explain (one summative per semester)	• *To Kill a Mockingbird* or *Of Mice and Men* • *A Long Way Gone* • Each unit and novel • *Animal Farm* or *To Kill a Mockingbird* and *Romeo and Juliet*
Draw evidence from literary or informational texts to support analysis, reflection, and research.	• I can use the text to support my written claim. • I can organize my ideas in written form according to the task.	• Character analysis • Theme analysis • Claim, Support, Explain (at least one formative per unit) • Claim, Support, Explain (one summative per semester)	• *To Kill a Mockingbird* or *Of Mice and Men* • *A Long Way Gone* • Each unit and novel • *Animal Farm* or *To Kill a Mockingbird* and *Romeo and Juliet*
Speak and present findings and supporting evidence with clear and coherent reasoning, development, organization, and style appropriate to task, purpose, and audience; evaluate and analyze a speaker's point of view, reasoning, and use of evidence and rhetoric, which may include digital media.	• I can clearly present information according to the task. • I can organize a presentation using digital media. • I can analyze a speaker's purpose.	• Formal and informal presentations on assigned topics • Chapter presentations evaluating textual evidence • Informal presentations connecting to historical context	• *To Kill a Mockingbird*, *Animal Farm*, or *The Odyssey* • *To Kill a Mockingbird* or *A Long Way Gone* • *To Kill a Mockingbird* or *Animal Farm*

Priority Standard	Learning Targets *I can* statements	Methods of Assessment How will students show what they know?	Pacing and Instructional Considerations Where does this appear in my curriculum?
Read and determine both explicit and inferential meaning, as well as cite textual evidence to support the argument or claim.	• I can cite evidence from the text to support what the text means. • I can draw inferences from the text.	• Annotate texts or close readings on significant portions from texts (formative and summative assessments) • Cite evidence while discussing text or answering written questions (quick writes or class discussions)	• *The Odyssey* and *Animal Farm* • *Of Mice and Men, To Kill a Mockingbird, Animal Farm, The Odyssey, A Long Way Gone, Romeo and Juliet*
Read and determine central ideas or themes, and analyze their development; summarize the key supporting details and ideas.	• I can analyze how a theme develops. • I can identify the plot. • I can determine how a plot develops. • I can summarize the key details in a text.	• Five-paragraph theme analysis • Analyze theme development (formative) • Identify plot development (formative) • Summarize supporting details in a short story (formative)	• *A Long Way Gone* • *The Odyssey* • *Of Mice and Men* • Short stories from Holt textbook
Read and interpret words and phrases as they are used in a text, including figurative and connotative meanings.	• I can define and identify figurative language in a text.	• Define and identify specific literary terms for each unit	• *Of Mice and Men, To Kill a Mockingbird, Animal Farm, The Odyssey, A Long Way Gone, Romeo and Juliet*

Source: © 2015 Traci Cox, Chelsea Dodds, and Dennis Ryan, Stillwater Junior High School, Stillwater, Minnesota. Used with permission.

Figure 2.6: First draft of priority standards and assessment plan for grade 9 English.

Two other teams—a grade 1 math team and a grade 7 science team—followed a similar process but with a twist. These teams had already done the work of teasing out the learning targets that aligned with each of their standards. They evaluated the standards and corresponding learning targets and navigated through the filtering process of placing those standards in categories: *essential to know, important to know,* and *nice to know.* Not all standards carry the same weight, and using the five criteria listed earlier in this section and outlined in figure 2.4 (page 39) will assist educators. Figure 2.7 (page 44) illustrates the categories of standards the teams identified.

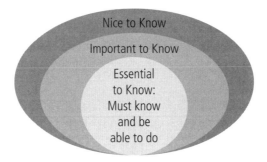

Figure 2.7: Categories of standards.

Because these teacher teams were also experts in their content areas, they struggled to narrow their focus. Their personal passions, interests, and experiences greatly impacted their individual advocacy for the particular standards to include or not include in their teams' list of what was most essential. This advocacy primarily related to thinking about what these teams always knew to be true about what they teach and when they teach it, as opposed to intentionally reflecting on the prioritization criteria. However, the power of process became evident. As the conversations began, the teams circled back to the criteria for selecting a common set of priority standards and could soon speak with one voice about their decisions—what their decisions were and why they made the decisions—in order to ensure success for each student. Figures 2.8 and 2.9 feature the teams' artifacts as they made these decisions.

By the end of first grade, 100 percent of students will:

- Count to 120 by ones, fives, and tens

- Count to 30 by twos

- Count forward and backward from any number up to 120

- Read any given number up to 120

- Write any given number up to 120

- Identify, name, and tell the value of all coins

- Count various combinations of pennies, nickels, and dimes

- Identify place value to the hundreds using the names *hundreds*, *tens*, and *ones*

- Tell time to the hour and half hour

- Solve story problems using a variety of strategies

- Demonstrate fact fluency: +0, +1,–0,–1, doubles up to 10 + 10, and sums of 10

- Find the missing addend (Example: _____ + 3 = 5)

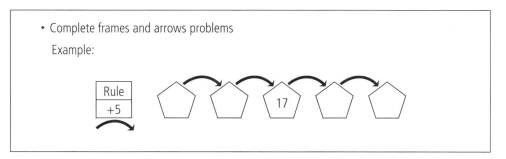

- Complete frames and arrows problems

    Example:

Source: © 2015 Nikki Anderson, Erica Bryant, Michelle Capelle, Kelsey Mueller, Marie Neher, Riverside Central Elementary School, Rochester, Minnesota. Used with permission.

Figure 2.8: Grade 1 mathematics priority standards.

Priority standards are the most essential skills and knowledge students need to know in order to progress in the discipline. The teacher will be intentional about assessing the priority standards, and if the students do not show mastery of these, the teacher will intervene.

Students in seventh-grade science will be able to:

- Understand that scientists learn about the natural world in a logical way that is testable and repeatable

- Understand that matter is made up of atoms that combine to make molecules, which provide the basis for understanding the properties of matter (periodic table organization and chemical equations)

- Distinguish the differences and similarities among plant, animal, and bacterial cells and recognize that cells divide to make more cells for growth and repair (cell processes too)

- Recognize and describe how the organs in the respiratory, circulatory, digestive, nervous, skin, and urinary systems interact to serve the needs of humans

- Understand that reproduction is a characteristic of all organisms and is essential for the continuation of a species, and hereditary information is contained in genes, which are inherited through sexual or asexual reproduction (sex cell formation, selective breeding)

- Recognize that individual organisms with certain traits in particular environments are more likely than others to survive and have offspring (fossils, variation, and extinction)

- Recognize that different microorganisms and viruses can cause specific diseases and that the human immune system responds to those disease-causing agents (vaccinations and medications)

- Understand the flow of energy and the recycling of matter and how they are essential to a stable ecosystem (photosynthesis/respiration and food webs/pyramids)

- Compare and contrast the roles and relationships among organisms (predator/prey, parasite/host, producers, consumers, and decomposers) in a specific ecosystem with the aid of graphs of predator and prey and maps of populations, and explain how organism populations are influenced by biotic and abiotic factors

Source: © 2015 Traci Cox, Pete Fuglestad, Vince Carlson, and Bretta Chaplinski, Stillwater Junior High School, Stillwater, Minnesota. Used with permission.

Figure 2.9: Grade 7 science priority standards.

We want to acknowledge and honor a specific point of pride from one of these teams as they were creating their common set of priority standards. A team member made an important revelation during the prioritizing conversation. As the team finalized its first draft, this team member shared the following reflection.

"So . . . I have this unit that I just love to teach. It's an area of interest for me, and my students' engagement is so high during this unit of study because they can see how passionate I am about it. But after going through this process, I realized that I was the only one teaching this unit. I also realized that the way I had been organizing my lessons did not at all align to the rigor of the standards, let alone even align to many of the standards themselves. You know . . . I think I have to let that unit go until I can make sure that I'm preparing students for what we've agreed is truly most essential. It's not easy for me to say, but it's what needs to happen for our team and our students."

Difficult team decisions require consensus. This team effectively worked through its disagreements on the most essential pieces of its content and, most important, committed to implementing what it collectively agreed on. To that end, you may think, "Well, if choosing the most essential standards is not that easy, then why can't my district or local education agency identify the essential learning for me? That way, I can make sure that I teach what I'm supposed to and that all students are successful." People ask us this question every place we go. We know that it comes from every teacher's strong desire to simply do the right thing and do it well. The hard truth is that this approach—while certainly desirable to some—is not practical or sustainable. Owning the work and the struggle to produce that work has great value. The group will feel more comfortable making adjustments as it gains feedback from its students while delivering the content. If the finished set of priority standards had instead been handed to them, the first struggle they experienced after adopting the standards might have resulted in some saying the work was not doable or possible with their students. Refer back to figure 2.2 (pages 32–33) for a tool to help foster the process of reaching consensus around a common set of priority standards.

Ponder Box

Take a moment to jot down or draw your initial thoughts about how your team's process for reaching consensus on priority standards compares to what we have described. Consider the following question as a team: Why do we need this information, and how will it advance our work? You can refer back to these notes later in the chapter as you and your teammates begin to work through the next section of the conversation.

Common Scope and Sequence

Previously, we alluded to the significant variability that exists in a student's academic experience when a guaranteed and viable curriculum is not present. Once educators have identified the most essential content for students to master, they can begin to map out their curriculum to ensure adequate time for students to learn that content. This common scope and sequence promotes accountability for what content educators should highly monitor and respond to but allows for flexibility in how they deliver content and how students engage with that content. Mapping the curriculum leads to heightened team clarity regarding what students should know and be able to do. It gives teams the opportunity to be intentional in their design for how they will naturally embed assessment and instructional agility in the learning framework (Schimmer, 2016). As teams focus their work around establishing a common scope and sequence, they aim to answer the question, What is the plan to make sure each team member works so that every student acquires the knowledge and skills that are most essential for the unit of study?

Heidi Hayes Jacobs has long been a lead researcher and developer of mapping strategies, tools, and resources to aid teachers in planning a common scope and sequence for their course or subjects within a grade level. She and Ann Johnson present a strong argument for teachers to learn about the *why* behind this process:

> We map to solve teaching and learning problems in a specific school setting. The most common problems that mappers address have remained fundamentally the same, though the implications have evolved. We use our maps . . . to gain information; replace repetition with spiraling classroom experiences; analyze gaps in student learning and mend them in the maps; align to standards; integrate natural curricular connections between disciplines and classrooms; update our maps on a regular basis for timelines, given the proliferation of knowledge; and stay vigilant in our quest for internal coherence in the map. (Jacobs & Johnson, 2009, p. 2)

Jacobs and Johnson's (2009) suggestions assist teachers in developing proficiency maps in order to understand the yearlong scope and sequence. Some questions to consider as teachers work through this planning are:

- How can we collaboratively define our yearlong plan for this course or subject?

- When do we expect proficiency of each standard? What level of proficiency is necessary at which points throughout the year?

- How many days are we willing to allot for each unit of study?

- Do we have congruence and alignment for students to have adequate opportunities to acquire mastery of the priority standards?

A team can accomplish this work in a variety of ways. The most important aspect of this work happens before the team even begins to dialogue about its instructional framework and design. We assert that the team must understand the connection between creating a common scope and sequence across the team and building a guaranteed and viable curriculum for students. If not all team members understand the relevance of the work, they may quickly revert back to compliance rather than champion a collective commitment to student achievement and growth.

A yearlong planning template can help students' parents and administrators review the scope and sequence for expected learning. The example in figure 2.10 is intentionally simple, in that it maps out the content rather than details specific assessments or strategies for measuring mastery. The intent is for teachers to acknowledge which standards they will present in which quarters. We recommend that you bold your priority standards to ensure that you give students multiple opportunities and varied learning activities over the course of the year to master the most essential content.

Academic Quarter	Reading: Informational	Reading: Literature	Language	Speaking and Listening	Writing
Quarter 1					
Quarter 2					
Quarter 3					
Quarter 4					

Figure 2.10: Yearlong literacy scope and sequence planning tool.

From this template, teachers can map out their curricular plans in greater detail. Consider part of a quarterly map for kindergarten literacy pacing that Angie created in her work with one district (see figure 2.11). Even at the end of the school year, these teacher teams work systematically to ensure opportunities for every student to achieve the expected levels of mastery.

Week in Quarter 4	Reading: Informational Text	Reading: Literature	Language	Writing
Week 33	RI.K.1 With prompting and support, ask and answer questions about key details in a text. RI.K.7 With prompting and support, describe the relationship between illustrations and the text in which they appear (for example, what person, place, thing, or idea in the text an illustration depicts).	RI.K.5 Recognize common types of texts (for example, storybooks, poems). RL.K.7 With prompting and support, describe the relationship between illustrations and the story in which they appear (for example, what moment in a story an illustration depicts).	L.K.2c Write a letter or letters for most consonant and short-vowel sounds. L.K.1e Use the most frequently occurring prepositions (for example, *to*, *from*, *in*, *out*, *on*, *off*, *for*, *of*, *by*, *with*).	W.K.3 Use a combination of drawing, dictating, and writing to narrate a single event or several loosely linked events, tell about the events in the order in which they occurred, and provide a reaction to what happened.
Week 34	RI.K.5 Identify the front cover, back cover, and title page of a book.		L.K.2a Capitalize the first word in a sentence and the pronoun *I*.	
Week 35		RL.K.5 Recognize common types of texts (for example, storybooks, poems).	L.K.2c Write a letter or letters for most consonant and short-vowel sounds. L.K.1c Form regular plural nouns orally by adding /s/ or /es/. L.K.1e Use the most frequently occurring prepositions (for example, *to*, *from*, *in*, *out*, *on*, *off*, *for*, *of*, *by*, *with*).	

Source for standards: Adapted from NGA & CCSSO, 2010.

Figure 2.11: Sample fourth-quarter scope and sequence planning tool.

As teachers consider their responsibility to resolve the teaching and learning challenges presented in their classrooms, it is important to capitalize on the moments *during* the learning process to intervene, adjust, and address any student misconceptions in order to move students to proficiency. Having instructional agility means having the ability to respond in the moment to the needs that students demonstrate (Schimmer, 2016). It means having enough confidence in what proficiency looks like—and what mile markers are on that road to proficiency—to quickly identify when student thinking is going off course and when to provide corrective instruction to get students back on track during learning. We will discuss this idea in more detail in chapter 5, but it is important to keep this in mind when determining scope and sequence. Teachers cannot demonstrate instructional agility if their curricular framework is so rigid that they cannot give students multiple opportunities to learn or to experience moments where learning can be enriched once they realize proficiency. That is not the kind of educational experience our students deserve.

Kim Bailey, Chris Jakicic, and Jeanne Spiller (2014) offer curricular planning support via a pacing guide. They define *pacing guide* as "a thoughtfully planned and designed sequence of teaching and learning that outlines specific learning targets to be addressed within a grading period or unit of instruction" (Bailey et al., 2014, p. 93). It is not intended to create rigid structures for teaching where every team member needs to stay on the same page on the same day. It is intended to help teachers understand what should be taught and learned within a certain window of time while also allowing for flexibility for appropriate differentiation or intervention when some students continue to demonstrate difficulty. Individual teachers may find this dance problematic, as they often struggle between when to move on and when to slow down. When the *team* collaboratively develops the pacing guide, however, it creates greater commitment to prioritizing the standards. This team development provides clarity in instructional focus with sound learning progressions, resulting in strong alignment of formative and summative assessments to measure students' levels of performance. Think what power this practice could have if pacing guides were then developed across the entire school! Vertically aligned pacing guides reduce the gaps in learning from year to year or course to course, prevent instructional overlaps, and enable all teachers to see how the rigor of the standards progresses over the span of students' academic experience.

Ponder Box

Take a moment to jot down or draw your initial thoughts about common scope and sequence. Consider the following questions as a team. You can refer back to these notes later in the chapter as you and your teammates begin to work through the next section of the conversation.

- How will our decisions impact the system to create greater balance and alignment?

- How will we know our impact?

Intentional Planning

The practice of seeking evidence of student learning is highly collaborative, and it depends on the engagement and investment of all team members. Nothing about this work lives in a silo. Educators will not be asked to engage in reflective dialogue and collective practice with their teams only to return to their individual classrooms and function independently from the agreements and commitments made by the team. An important challenge to address is simply making a plan to get started. In chapter 1, we asked you to reflect on practices for creating norms, building trust, and fostering healthy relationships among your team. Now that you have established beliefs and behaviors that honor the elements of trust, respect, and collaboration, we invite you to discuss your first steps to guide this transformational change at the team level.

As a team, begin to ask each other:

- What student work sampling will certify that my students know the content to the level I need them to know it?

- How will my teammates and I work collaboratively to clarify our expectations for what success looks like?

- How will we make students aware of our expectations and give them feedback along their pathway to content mastery?

These are some of the critical decisions we face as we design the ways students will demonstrate what they've learned. Let's start thinking through these decisions and design a process for how our collaborative work can better ascertain the impact our instructional delivery has on our students.

Use figure 2.12 (page 53) to explore the initial key factors for promoting a guaranteed and viable curriculum. The Supporting Research column highlights fundamental considerations from experts in the field. At the end of this tool, we include a list of driving resources from these thought leaders, which you may wish to consult. Link the key factors with the supporting research to analyze practices and processes within your organization through the lenses of the current state, desired achievements, and interrupting practices.

Concluding Thoughts to Heighten Systems Thinking

This chapter has introduced you to some important aspects of seeking evidence as we build an Unstoppable Assessment system. When we learn something new—or prepare to embark on a new challenge—we often have a level of excitement that energizes and invigorates us but simultaneously hinders our ability to clearly see the best course of action. It's hard to temper the feeling of wanting to do it all right now! We recommend you complete the templates in figures 2.1–2.3 (pages 30–35) and 2.12. After you reflect on your current reality and consider the manner in which this work will strengthen your learning system as a whole, refer to the reproducible "Seeking Evidence Systems Protocol" (page 55). Complete the protocol as a team *prior* to reading the next chapter to maximize your collaborative work and advance your team's growth. As you reflect on what this chapter affirmed, what you learned, and what may have given you pause, also use the reproducible template "Focusing Our View Within the System: Seeking Evidence" (page 56) to acknowledge your thoughts before moving forward.

Subject area or department: _____   Team members: _____

Key Factors What composes a guaranteed and viable curriculum?	Supporting Research What do experts say about the value and purpose of this work?	Current State What do our practices and processes look like now?	Desired Achievements What do we want our success—in both practice and process—to look like?	Interrupting Practices What behaviors shut down thinking or hinder progress as we engage in our work?
Collaborative Team Structures and Processes	• Require regular meetings that are focused only on student learning • Create high levels of trust between group members, allowing for productive conflict as a means to consensus and commitment • Seek to identify and enhance instructional practices that work, evidenced by student work sampling and data • Create shared ownership among team members for the success of all students while allowing them to see themselves as interdependent			
Common Set of Priority Standards by Course	• Identifies the priority or big ideas of the curriculum and standards for each grade level, course, and content area (fewer than ten per semester) • Lists essential standards based on the following criteria: endurance, leverage, and readiness • Promotes clarity among the team on the most essential content to be learned • Allows a team to plan its common formative and summative assessment work around these priority standards • Helps establish a curriculum that can be taught in the time allowed • Reflects what teachers will commit to intervene on when students don't know it yet			

continued →

Figure 2.12: Championing Unstoppable Assessment systems—Guaranteed and viable curriculum.

Key Factors What composes a guaranteed and viable curriculum?	Supporting Research What do experts say about the value and purpose of this work?	Current State What do our practices and processes look like now?	Desired Achievements What do we want our success—in both practice and process—to look like?	Interrupting Practices What behaviors shut down thinking or hinder progress as we engage in our work?
Common Scope and Sequence by Course	• Is supported by studies that have shown it could take up to twenty-three years to cover all standards that have been established at national and state levels • Promotes greater consistency in what is taught, regardless of who is teaching the class, by clarifying what standards mean and what they look like and sound like in classrooms • Establishes common pacing as a prerequisite for common formative assessments • Promotes vertical alignment and articulation of what curriculum is actually being implemented, versus what is intended			

Thought Leaders and Driving Resources

DuFour, R., DuFour, R., Eaker, R., Many, T. W., & Mattos, M. (2016). *Learning by doing: A handbook for Professional Learning Communities at Work* (3rd ed.). Bloomington, IN: Solution Tree Press.

Fullan, M. (2005). *Leadership and sustainability: System thinkers in action.* Thousand Oaks, CA: Corwin Press.

Graham, P., & Ferriter, W. M. (2010). *Building a Professional Learning Community at Work: A guide to the first year.* Bloomington, IN: Solution Tree Press.

Hattie, J. (2009). *Visible learning: A synthesis of over 800 meta-analyses relating to achievement.* New York: Routledge.

Marzano, R. J. (2003). *What works in schools: Translating research into action.* Alexandria, VA: Association for Supervision and Curriculum Development.

Reeves, D. (Ed.). (2007). *Ahead of the curve: The power of assessment to transform teaching and learning.* Bloomington, IN: Solution Tree Press.

Seeking Evidence Systems Protocol

Team Members: _____ Date: _____

Unit or Topic of Study: _____

Zoom In	*What kind of information do we need to ensure all students experience a learning environment that enables them to attain high levels of achievement?*	
	What is the innovative idea that brings relevance and meaning to this unit for students?	
	What are the priority standards that will be addressed in this unit of study?	
	What student misconceptions do we anticipate along the learning pathway to achieving mastery of these skills or concepts?	

Zoom Out	*How does our assessment design marry with our instructional framework to enable all students to achieve the desired results?*		
	Essential Standards or Learning Targets Addressed	Possible Methods of Assessment with Appropriate Rigor	Supporting Learning Tasks and Activities

Panoramic	*How do we partner with students to seek the evidence we desire?*		
	Days in the Unit Sequence	Embedded Assessment (Formative or Summative)	Type of Student Feedback Loop or Reflection

Assessing Unstoppable Learning © 2018 Solution Tree Press • SolutionTree.com
Visit **go.SolutionTree.com/assessment** to download this free reproducible.

Focusing Our View Within the System:
Seeking Evidence

Zoom In	**Zoom Out**
What is our current reality? What kind of information are we looking for to move us toward the results we desire?	Why do we need this information? How will it advance our work?
Panoramic	**View From Above**
How will these decisions or conversations impact our system? What is the potential to create greater balance and alignment within?	How will we leverage the gifts and talents of the people within the system to heighten systems thinking throughout?

CHAPTER 3

GATHERING EVIDENCE TO USE ASSESSMENT AS INSTRUCTION

It's hard to address rigorous standards without a plan. It's equally hard to ensure that students develop mastery if we don't assess them.

—Douglas Fisher and Nancy Frey

The increased rigor of the academic standards—and the ensuing expectations for what students should be able to do with what we have taught them—is not breaking news. Well-intended state, provincial, and national mandates for accountability have resulted in the unfortunate consequence of breaking our curriculum apart to monitor every discrete skill and measure anything and everything within our reach. This has given rise to a need for balanced and coherent assessment systems that will provide a more realistic and holistic approach to proficiency—and the learning progressions that will guide students there—and monitor student progress before, during, and after the learning process. Schimmer (2016) discusses this balance as a means for educators to "understand and maximize the role of assessment for feedback (formative) and assessment for verification (summative)" (p. 12). Richard Stiggins, Judith Arter, Jan Chappuis, and Stephen Chappuis (2004) similarly refer to formative assessment as *assessment* for *learning* and refer to summative assessment as *assessment* of *learning*. Schimmer (2016) further asserts, "We know that there are typically more practices than games, more rehearsals than performances; likewise, balance doesn't mean a 1:1 ratio of formative to summative—it means we effectively use both" (p. 12).

Educators collectively, however, have yet to systematically work together in every building and every district to clarify what mastery looks like and how it will be achieved. Although we understand this cautious approach, we submit that collaborative frameworks that ensure every teacher has a clear understanding of what student competence looks like and sounds like—and what application and relevance the content has outside the school learning environment—can facilitate the systematic work that needs to occur.

Gathering evidence assists systems thinking educators as they make sense of what students need to know and at what level they need to know it (think back to your reflections in chapter 2). We must honor educators by accommodating these collaborative structures and processes in order to determine a course of action for teaching and learning that allows each student access to the information *and* a deep understanding of what success will look like. The challenge comes in developing a plan that provides time for teachers to teach, for students to learn, and for teachers to react—with either corrective instruction or extension—in response to what evidence students display. In this chapter, we will share an assessment design frame—or architecture (Erkens, Schimmer, & Vagle, 2017)—that reflects a way to foster that synergy among teacher teams to accurately determine the criteria for success via intentional assessment and curricular and instructional design.

In this chapter, we will discuss the following essential items to consider and include as you develop a balanced assessment plan as a team: understanding balanced assessment, clarifying assessment types and purposes, utilizing summative and formative assessments effectively, leveraging cognitive rigor, designing accurate assessments, and applying project-based learning. At **go.SolutionTree.com /assessment**, we also offer an extensive exemplar of one team's assessment design work as an online supplement to this chapter.

- **Zoom in:** What is the expected level of performance at this point in the lesson or unit? How do we collect, manage, and organize our student work in order to effectively represent what our students know and can do as well as what they haven't learned just yet?

- **Zoom out:** How will our assessment design—and corollary instructional plans—enable us to give timely, descriptive feedback to students about what they can do with what we've been teaching them?

- **Panoramic:** How will we prepare to report our evidence in order to efficiently discuss it with our colleagues and our students?

Understanding Balanced Assessment

Before we discuss the items to consider as you develop an assessment plan to gather evidence of student learning, it's important we ensure that teams are on the same page as to what balanced assessment entails and what effective balanced assessment systems look like. Assessment is not separate from instruction. Assessment is not an event. Rather, through intentionality, clarified purpose, direct instruction, and descriptive feedback, educators harmonize assessment design with instructional agility to elicit the right kind of evidence from students at the right times during learning.

Ponder Box

Reflect on your current understanding of a balanced assessment system. How can such a system enhance students' levels of learning and bring partnership between them and their teachers? Jot down or draw your initial thoughts or questions for reflection.

In the spirit of learning being a process—a journey, rather than a destination—teacher teams need a solid understanding of what learning should look like at the end of each unit of study and the end of each course or grade level. Fisher and Frey (2015) remind us that

> we further activate students' learning by helping them weigh what it is they already know against the larger goals or outcomes for the unit through the use of anticipatory activities, such as demonstrations, discrepant events, visual displays, and thought-provoking questions. (p. 9)

Despite the enormous body of research cited throughout this text, which echoes our assertions about the power of quality assessment design, our personal experience and our conversations with educators reveal that much undergraduate coursework for aspiring teachers continues to place heavier emphasis on the elements of effective teaching, such as using high-yield instructional strategies, in order to achieve the results we desire from our students. A glaring absence continues to be specific training and practice for teachers to develop and grow their capacity to determine what a student may have actually *learned* from their teaching. Some teachers base their lessons' success solely on whether the students were engaged, had fun, or completed the intended project or task. Let us be clear; we place great value on teachers intentionally planning an engaging idea to hook learners into the content delivery. We see great importance in teachers aspiring to have classrooms filled with students who see the connections between their schoolwork and college or career readiness and who become deeply invested in their learning. We also expect our teachers to have worked with their teams to collectively determine what learning looks like and sounds like in those classrooms. Kay Burke (2010) reminds us that assessment is the manner in which we are "gathering evidence of student learning to inform instructional decisions," whereas with evaluation, we are "collecting information and making a judgment about it" (p. 19). Making this distinction is essential to your team's planning and the process by which you will determine to what level students know and can do something with the information you have taught them.

To help visualize this distinction, review the sample balanced assessment model in figure 3.1. A teacher we collaborated with shared this exemplar, which she uses in her geometry course (E. Fisher, personal communication, July 2016). It includes suggestions for grading, which she discusses with her students. Her system starts with the creation of a final chapter test in order to review the learning targets addressed, and then she builds intentional moments throughout the instruction for that chapter to monitor students' progress. We like this example because it models the systems thinking approach of marrying assessment and instruction, and it honors multiple opportunities for students to demonstrate their thinking as they work toward mastery. Notice how classwork and homework are used in tandem with the other components yet are not considered part of the student's final grade. As this teacher notes, "Learning is still taking place." Additionally, access "Putting It All Together: Geometry Exemplar" at **go.SolutionTree.com/assessment** for a detailed illustration of the process her team uses to design balanced assessments.

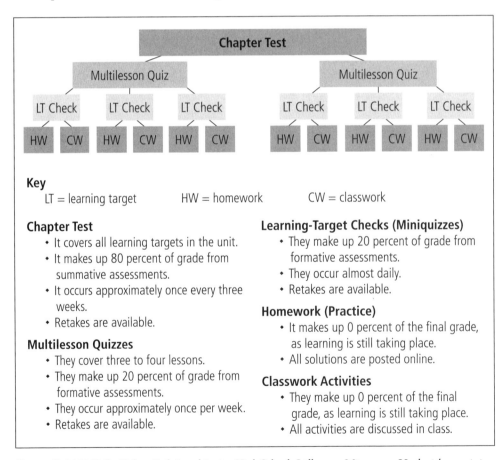

Source: © 2015 Erika Fisher, Oak-Land Junior High School, Stillwater, Minnesota. Used with permission.

Figure 3.1: Sample summative assessment model breakdown.

Ponder Box

Consider the following question as a team: What are our current practices for gathering evidence of learning from students?

Another district we worked with rejuvenated one of its evaluation methods—the report card—to better honor students' demonstration of learning for mastery and move away from the previous model of compliance. Gone are the days when a student could bring in a box of facial tissues for five extra points to get that A at the end of the term. Instead, those days have been replaced with a model of true understanding of the most essential content to learn, coupled with clear, consistent criteria by which that learning will be reported. The revised standards-based report card accurately communicates a student's level of mastery around a particular standard at the time that mastery occurs. Students then have opportunities to advance beyond mastery of the standard when they are ready. In a separate section on the report card titled Learner Attributes, the student gets recognition for the dispositions of character that enhance his or her ability to contribute and persevere through the struggles brought forward during the learning process.

In this district, the learner attributes reported align with the 4Cs—21st century skills—of collaboration, communication, critical thinking, and creative problem solving (Partnership for 21st Century Learning, n.d.). We need to ensure students learn the academic content required to set the stage for them to answer bigger questions like the following.

- How will my knowledge and contributions change the world?

- If we know that we will report on our students' ability to collaborate, what possibilities for assessments allow students to work in partnership to demonstrate what they collectively know?

- What benefits come from presenting students with situations or scenarios they have not yet seen in order to determine to what level students can apply the skills and concepts we have taught?

- What value comes from giving students choice in how they represent their level of understanding of the content so they can communicate their learning in a style that allows for enhanced personalization of learning?

Ponder Box

Jot down or draw your thinking, wonderings, or ideas as you consider opportunities to engage students in learning activities and assessments that will prepare them for collaboration, communication, critical thinking, and creative problem solving. Where can these skills develop as students engage in learning experiences with their teachers?

Assessment design should acknowledge how learning occurs for students in the first place. In order to understand the kind of preparation needed to accurately assess students and their learning, let's take a moment to secure a common understanding of the various types and purposes of assessments that will support student mastery along the way.

Clarifying Assessment Types and Purposes

Summative and formative assessment measures of student learning have two key differences: (1) the number of learning targets teams assess and (2) how teams will use the information. The number of learning targets assessed will be greater on a summative assessment than on a formative assessment. Summative assessments that occur most often at the classroom level are end-of-course, benchmark, interim, end-of-unit, and chapter tests. The learning targets measured by these summative assessments often come from multiple standards.

Formative assessments have an equally valuable place in our assessment framework yet have a very different purpose from our summative measures. Because systems thinking educators have carefully designed their guaranteed and viable curriculum, including the intentional design of summative assessments, they can utilize information from common formative assessments to ascertain whether students are on track to master the most essential content. Formative assessments enable educators to monitor student learning on a timely basis, which provides more discrete feedback on which concepts are secure, which concepts need more support, and what misconceptions or errors are present so that corrective instruction can occur.

As we think about our methods of assessment—and the respective manners in which we seek evidence of learning from our students—we want to ensure students have an opportunity to show us what they know and to what level they know it. This requires us to first determine which type of assessment will give us information about both students' strengths and their next steps in learning. Although we know that whether a student got an answer right or wrong has value, can we stretch ourselves to seek information that tells us to what *level* a student knows something? Can we create tiered opportunities that allow our students to show us where they are on the learning continuum? A lot of learning space exists between *mastery* and *does not show mastery*. Educators must design an instructional space that gives students the opportunity to recognize where they fit on that continuum and gives them permission to be wherever they are without fear, anxiety, or debilitation. Our actions will give our students the confidence and inspiration they need to take their next steps toward learning for mastery.

Before educators can thoughtfully plan the assessments that occur throughout the various units of study, we need to recognize examples of these types of assessments. Fisher and Frey (2015) offer formal and informal examples of both formative and summative assessments (see table 3.1) we can use to assess our learners throughout the course of instruction.

Table 3.1: Examples of Different Assessment Types

	Formal	**Informal**
Formative	**Analytic writing inventory:** Group students for instruction, such as for voice, tone, or organization. **Validated skills inventory:** Assign online practice work to individual students.	**Check-in:** Listen to a group of students, and then provide a prompt based on the errors identified. **Written exit slips:** Plan future instruction of misunderstood concepts.
Summative	**End-of-unit exam:** Cover the unit's topic, and calculate a grade. **Group presentation:** Use a calibrated rubric to score student demonstration of knowledge.	**Online discussion board postings:** Use as part of a participation grade. **Notebook check:** Review a sampling of lecture notes, assignments, tasks, and reflections.

Source: Fisher & Frey, 2015, p. 11.

The majority of readers are likely familiar with common assessment terms. Yet, as Michael Fullan (2005) states, "Terms travel easily . . . but the meaning of the underlying concepts does not" (p. 67). Fisher and Frey (2015) offer a simple matrix to assist teachers in differentiating various types and purposes of assessments (see table 3.2, page 64). Any of these types may be used formatively or summatively. Refer to these throughout your assessment design journey as you consider the evidence that allows students to most accurately and authentically demonstrate their learning.

Table 3.2: Purpose Versus Procedure

Type	Purpose	Procedure
Norm-referenced tests	To measure a student's performance in a variety of skills and compare those scores to the scores of students in other geographic locations	Administered at set intervals; students answer questions from a booklet on standard forms (*or complete the assessment online*)
Criterion-referenced tests	To indicate attainment of mastery on specific instructional objectives, usually by answering a percentage of questions correctly	Administered with lesson plans; students read items and answer on separate paper (*or separate format*)
Teacher-made or publisher-made tests (such as true or false, fill in, multiple choice, or essay)	To measure retention and comprehension of specific content	Administered within lesson plan; students answer focused questions in various formats

Source: Adapted from Fisher & Frey, 2015, p. 91.

Many summative assessments from this matrix become required parts of a school district's evidence-gathering system that are essential in order to provide the systematic supports, guidance, materials, and resources (including time, space, and people) to move each student in the district to mastery. But without intentional communication about what they assess—and why they assess it—these district-, state-, or province-level assessments can be seen as nuisances and interruptions, rather than as assessments that provide an added value to the overall functionality of the district's curriculum, instruction, and assessment framework. Figure 3.2 features an assessment matrix Angie created upon entering Stillwater Area Public Schools in Stillwater, Minnesota, to help educators and families understand the purposes and intentions behind each of the various formal or standardized assessments administered over the course of a school year. By the time you read this book, this template will have gone through revisions in response to feedback from educators and families and to the new district leadership team's commitment to build systems for educators so they can actually interpret and use the student data they collect.

Before students can invest as partners in the learning process, educators need to clearly state why they are collecting evidence and let students know what they intend to do with that information. Students need to have meaningful and thoughtful answers to their two greatest questions: (1) Why do I have to learn this? and (2) What's the value of this for me? If students start to think, "Here we go again, another test," educators have an opportunity to communicate the value of assessment and its marriage to high-quality, personalized instruction that moves each student to mastery.

2015–2016 Stillwater Area Public Schools Assessment Matrix and Intent of Use
Updated October 2016

Evidence of Learning	Source	Formats	Timing	Targets	Intents	Sample Questions Answered
Running Records or Informal Reading Inventories	Teachers College, Columbia University	Administered 1:1 with teacher and student	September, May As needed to monitor progress	Reading, grades K–6	• Identify patterns in reading behavior • Determine appropriate levels of text for independent reading • Inform teaching	• How is a student using strategies to make meaning of words or the text as a whole? • What is the instructional reading level of this student? • How well is this student developing his or her reading skills and strategies over time?
Cognitive Abilities Test (CogAT Form 7) CogAT Overview	Riverside Publishing	Abilities assessment in verbal, nonverbal, and quantitative areas Grades 2–4 (paper)	November	Grades 2–5, with eligibility based on achievement scores	• Assess students' abilities in reasoning and problem solving using verbal, quantitative, and nonverbal (spatial) symbols • Screen for needs of gifted learners	• What are the student's learning reasoning and problem-solving skills? • How well does this student make inferences, demonstrate connections, and use cognitive resources in new situations?

Figure 3.2: Sample assessment matrix.

continued →

Evidence of Learning	Source	Formats	Timing	Targets	Intents	Sample Questions Answered
Minnesota Comprehensive Assessments (MCA) State Testing Information	Minnesota Department of Education	Mathematics: Untimed, online, multiple-choice questions, adaptive within the grade level Reading: Untimed, online, multiple-choice questions, adaptive within the grade level Science: Untimed, online, one test per level (elementary, junior high, and high school)	Reading: April 4–15* Mathematics: April 18–29* Science: May 2–13* *Each school will set its own schedule within this window.	Reading: Grades 3–8, 10 Mathematics: Grades 3–8, 11 Science: Grades 5, 8, 10	• Federal accountability • Summative • Measure student progress toward achieving Minnesota academic standards	• Is the district making adequate yearly progress toward all students achieving proficiency on academic standards? • Are students making adequate growth over time? • Is there evidence of progress toward closing achievement gaps? • What percentage of students are meeting grade-level standards?
ACT Plus Writing ACT Overview	American College Testing	Online	March 15	All grade 11 students (required by Minnesota Department of Education)	• College entrance • Career interests	• How have students progressed relative to college readiness? • Which college readiness benchmarks have students met? • Which students aren't ready for college, and in which areas are they struggling?

Utilizing Summative and Formative Assessments Effectively

With either assessment, the most critical aspect of gathering evidence remains knowing what to do with the information once we have it. In chapter 4, we will go into greater detail for discussing evidence as part of the Unstoppable Assessment framework. Our assessments need to reveal which students are in which place on the learning continuum and communicate the kinds of supports—intervention, monitoring, or extension—that will provide students with their respective next step.

Gathering evidence from students will prove ineffective in the absence of a plan. These moments in which we choose to gather information from students about what they know must occur at intentionally planned times for explicit purposes. Cassandra Erkens (2016) outlines an assessment map that teams can design for each unit of study as they match their instruction with their opportunities to gather evidence from students (see figure 3.3). This development allows each teacher on a team—as well as each student—to be crystal clear on the learning activities that will support content mastery.

Standard: **WHST.6–8.1** Write arguments focused on discipline-specific content.
Target 1: **WHST.6–8.1a** Introduce claims about a topic or issue, acknowledge and distinguish the claim(s) from alternate or opposing claims, and organize the reasons and evidence logically.
Target 2: **WHST.6–8.1b** Support claims with logical reasoning and relevant, accurate data and evidence that demonstrate an understanding of the topic or text, using credible sources.
Target 3: **WHST.6–8.1c** Use words, phrases, and clauses to create cohesion and clarify the relationships among claims, counterclaims, reasons, and evidence.
Target 4: **WHST.6–8.1d** Establish and maintain a formal style.
Target 5: **WHST.6–8.1e** Provide a concluding statement or section that follows from and supports the argument presented.
Assessments: (H) homework, (CRR) close read and response, (Q) quiz, paper, and essay exam

Target	H1	CRR1	H2	CRR2	Q1	H3	H4	Q2	CRR3	Paper	Exam
Target 1	1, 4, 6, 9, 10	Rubric	1–3					Rubric	Rubric	Scale	Scale
Target 2	2, 3, 5, 7, 8	Rubric	4–5		Rubric	Rubric			Rubric		
Target 3				Rubric			Rubric		Rubric		
Target 4				Rubric		Rubric	Rubric		Rubric		
Target 5		Rubric	6–10	Rubric		Rubric	Rubric	Rubric	Rubric		

Source: Erkens, 2016, p. 67; Adapted from NGA & CCSSO, 2010.

Figure 3.3: Secondary assessment map example.

Leveraging Cognitive Rigor

It's rare during our work with educators that we discover a team that has *not* yet gone through a process of reviewing its standards. Some educators refer to this review process as *unpacking standards*; others may use terms like *unwrapping, deconstructing,* or *decomposing*. No matter what your team names the process, it likely involves the essence of the following four steps.

1. **Circle the verbs:** These words describe how students need to show mastery.

2. **Underline the nouns or noun phrases:** These words define what students need to do to show mastery.

3. **Bracket the context:** These words define in what kind of setting or scenario students need to perform the task to demonstrate mastery.

4. **Identify learning targets:** These targets support students' understanding of the progression of learning required for mastery.

It's common to see teams, at the conclusion of this technical process, initiate the discussion on how to put this newly uncovered information into practice for students and implement changes in instructional design. For example, once teams reveal what students need to know and do in order to show mastery of standards, the next phase is for teams to reach a collective agreement on what proficiency looks like and sounds like relative to each standard. Too often, we encounter schools and districts that have varying levels of tolerance for what constitutes acceptable student performance. Classroom management processes or active monitoring of student behavioral expectations are common areas where this variance occurs. It is equally as imperative that "reads at grade level" in one classroom means the same thing in another. All educators across a grade level need to agree on what constitutes cognitive rigor, and common definitions and criteria regarding the quality of a lab report, an essay, or a constructed model must stay the same from classroom to classroom. When students have a clear target, they can meet the expectations required for mastery. If the expected levels of student performance vary between classrooms or between schools, this does a significant disservice to students. This lack of alignment results in students being ill prepared for their next levels of learning and some students having an inaccurate interpretation of what they need to do to best equip themselves for future challenges and opportunities.

Educators are experiencing a time when much of the instruction they provide to students has already been planned for them. Textbooks and programs come with prepackaged worksheets, graphic organizers, and resources as well as a scope and sequence to follow. We suggest that the convenience of these resources can run dangerously parallel to an unintentional absence of teacher-required *thinking* relative to the required levels of rigor for students. We assert that teachers must collaboratively make sense of how learning progressions need to unfold for student mastery to result. This essential practice for impacting student achievement requires that we intentionally welcome the words *rigor* and *relevance* into our collaborative conversations.

It can be daunting to invite these words into our assessment practice. Let's take a minute to unlearn the implications these words have had in our past practice and develop a common lens for how they can instead leverage student learning and advance teacher practice. Consider thoughts from our colleagues in table 3.3 as they make sense of these terms relative to practice.

Table 3.3: Reflections on Rigor and Relevance

Resource	Rigor	Relevance
Bailey et al. (2014)	"Rigor is the active learning on the part of the students and a strong connection between students and the *why* of the task. In other words, a driving problem or context helps to focus the students to not only become more knowledgeable about content but to apply and reflect on the result of that application" (pp. 142–143).	"When we use the term *relevance*, we're talking about the level of connection students will have to the content they are learning. It doesn't imply that they have personal experience . . . A task is considered relevant when students have a purpose for knowing" (p. 143).
Fisher & Frey (2015)	"Rigor is a combination of high standards and learner expectations paired with challenging task demands that result in student application of knowledge using critical-thinking skills within and across disciplines" (p. 51).	"Students want to know what they are expected to learn as well as how they are expected to demonstrate that learning. Perhaps even more importantly, they want to know why they should learn the content" (p. 52).
Vagle (2015)	"Quality rigorous tasks involve our students in taking the concepts we want them to learn and asking them to— individually or in collaboration with peers—evaluate, analyze, and problem solve" (pp. 45–46).	"Relevance involves application of concepts in different ways and situations. It is about generating wonder and interest in what we are asking students to learn" (p. 46).

Ponder Box

Given the definitions and interpretations of rigor and relevance presented in table 3.3 (page 69), jot down or draw your thinking in response. How do you make sense of rigor and relevance, and how will you incorporate these elements into your assessment practice and instructional delivery?

Embedding rigor and relevance into collaborative dialogue can help shift our assessment practice in the right direction. Understanding the cognitive rigor of a standard enables teacher teams to create assessment items or tasks where students can most accurately represent their thinking, understanding, or application of content.

Not every standard presents the same level of rigor. The learning progressions presented in the standards indicate differing levels of rigor that students will experience on their journey to mastery. Educators have expressed concerns over the gap that the increased rigor of the standards has meant for student achievement. They seem to play the game of catch-up with students each year in order to move all students to the new level that these standards have set. Educators worry—and rightfully so—whether students will be able to meet these high expectations. We believe that students *can* meet these benchmarks, and through informed teacher practice, they will.

The transfer of shared knowledge and understanding to the assessment *design* demonstrates our beliefs about what students can do with what we have taught them. Vagle (2015) shares:

> What we ask students to do through our assessment items and performance tasks speaks to what we believe students *can* do and is part of how we communicate expectations. . . . It is in the design of high-quality assessment tasks that we communicate these high expectations to students. . . . Student confidence is built through well-planned formative assessment practices and instruction that offers students time to practice, revise, and see and to experience growth on essential standards. (p. 45)

The larger question becomes, How will we know whether our teaching results in the level of rigor the standard requires? The answer lies in how we ask students to show us what they know through our intentional assessment design.

Designing Accurate Assessments

One team Angie worked with found great comfort in teaching the *topics* it had always taught and didn't want to go back and "redo" its work in order to align those topics to standards, nor did the team want to move away from its hundred-point, multiple-choice final exam. The team members did agree, however, that the manner in which they assessed didn't give them good information about what to do next in their instruction. They did not design their questions to the rigor of the standards, nor did they note the standards they assessed anywhere on their final exam. But the textbook claimed to be standards based, so the team concluded that everything in the textbook must consist of aligned, valid, and reliable ways in which to gather information about what students know. However, this team also agreed that students weren't too sure what their results meant, other than their alignment to a mark in the gradebook.

This team's story represents a common theme that has come up among hundreds of educators with whom we have worked. The team members believed they did what they were supposed to. Their district had provided them with a curriculum, and they were supposed to teach it. Although we know that the district appreciated the team members' fidelity to the curriculum they received, this team (and potentially the district office) had misinterpreted the value of adult collaboration and critical thinking as part of the teaching and learning process. However, the team members' collaborative conversations did help them begin to identify areas for improvement in their assessments, which they could then address through intentional assessment design. When teachers plan together, they collectively determine and agree on the intended outcomes of the lessons they teach.

Ensuring accurate assessment design can effectively leverage teachers' ability to deeply understand a student's next steps in his or her learning. It enables teachers to thoughtfully coordinate and utilize information from assessments to accurately determine what a student *does* know as well as which areas he or she still finds difficult to master. Cassandra Erkens, Tom Schimmer, and Nicole Dimich Vagle (2017) remind us that assessment architecture becomes most effective when it is planned, purposeful, and intentionally sequenced in advance of instruction by all those responsible for its delivery. These authors push teachers to seek clarity around what they do in their classrooms, why they do it, and who can gain the most from it. Although many elements of our organizations may be out of our reach to revitalize, we *can* control the manner in which our team functions as we strive to create this rich, intentionally articulated teaching and learning experience for our students. But be advised: this may mean stretching ourselves beyond what we have always known to be true about the manner in which we plan for and execute our craft and our passion. To review a detailed example of one team's assessment design process for a unit of study, visit **go.SolutionTree.com/assessment** to access "Putting It All Together: Geometry Exemplar."

Applying Project-Based Learning

In his book *Transforming Schools Using Project-Based Learning, Performance Assessment, and Common Core Standards*, Bob Lenz (2015) helps us more practically understand the necessity for students to do more than respond to questions we ask of them about the content we teach. *Project-based learning* is a teaching and learning strategy whereby students gain knowledge and skills by investigating and responding to an authentic, engaging, and complex question, problem, or challenge. Lenz (2015) highlights this distinction by using the pursuit of a driver's license as an example. Each individual must complete two assessments before receiving the coveted certification to cruise freely and independently on the road. One test—the driver's permit exam—is a written test that one must pass before he or she is even allowed to practice driving. Few people would call demonstrating mastery of the rules of the road in writing a trivial matter. Yet none of us received our official driver's license without also spending a significant number of hours practicing our application of those rules by getting behind the wheel and *driving*—on a real road, with other drivers vying for lane space, and with all the other distractions that come with that experience. We would never conclude that an individual who only passed the permit test has adequately prepared to drive independently and without restriction. The final performance, which includes being observed while *actually* driving on the road, earns each individual his or her official license.

Lenz (2015) connects this practical example to our practices in education. He states:

> Our K–12 education system has much to learn from such common sense. We give our students lots of permit exams and hardly any driver's tests. We measure (or attempt to measure) what they know, hoping it serves as a proxy for what they can do. The upshot is that many young adults leave high school unprepared to drive the metaphoric roads of college or career. (p. 42)

Michael McDowell is superintendent of Ross School District in Ross, California, and a firm believer in using project-based learning (PBL) as an effective way to tap into the knowledge students possess while providing them with an alternate format to demonstrate it. His book *Rigorous PBL by Design* (2017) speaks to some key shifts in PBL. In PBL, the project is the teaching strategy. Students learn the desired outcomes *through* the project rather than by being taught in another mode and then completing a project. McDowell (2017) proposes four key phases for projects.

1. **Project launch:** Teachers introduce students to the transfer-level learning expectations of the project. At the transfer level, students apply basic and complex understanding and skills to challenging problems within and between contexts. Learners can link ideas in new ways and make predictions, evaluations, and generalizations across contexts.

2. **Surface workshops:** Students learn surface-level information, complete surface-level tasks, and receive instruction at the surface level. At the surface level, students understand single or multiple ideas; the connections they make between ideas and to the larger principle or skill set is limited.

3. **Deeper workshops:** Students learn deeper-level information, complete deeper-level tasks, and receive deeper-level instruction. At the deeper level, learners relate multiple ideas and understand similarities and differences among concepts and skills. Moreover, learners understand how specific ideas are related to the underlying principles of a discipline.

4. **Presentations and reflections:** Students present their understanding of surface- and deeper-level outcomes and create transfer-level solutions. Students also reflect on their learning.

McDowell (2017) includes a number of project ideas in his book, including a high school social studies and English language arts project titled "Changing or Maintaining Our Imperialist Imperative." The project focuses students on understanding the significant impact industrialized nations have on developing nations. It addresses military, social, and economic reasons for industrialized nations to interact with and fundamentally influence other nations, and the positive and negative impacts those relationships have on the involved parties. Figure 3.4 illustrates a planning template teachers can use when implementing PBL, using this project as an example.

Project Design		
Learning Intentions	The industrialized nations' desire for abundant resources and new markets for their goods, coupled with feelings of cultural superiority (such as social Darwinism) and increased military power, allowed for and encouraged imperial expansion. Imperialism had lasting positive and negative effects.	
Success Criteria		
Surface	Deep	Transfer
• The student understands there were political, economic, and social reasons that drove European countries to take over other nations.	• The student analyzes the causes, characteristics, and effects of 19th century European imperialism, making evaluations of specific countries' imperialistic actions.	• The student analyzes historians' written assessments of the era and draws conclusions and infers possible outcomes as they relate to similar geopolitical actions today. • The student analyzes the present-day legacy of imperialism in at least one region of the world.

Figure 3.4: Sample PBL project-design template.

continued →

Driving Questions	How do the United States and other industrialized imperial nations prevent creating new global enemies?
Contexts	• ISIS • Global trade • Economic sanctions

Tasks		
Surface	**Deep**	**Transfer**
Address the following in pairs and with the class: • Identify conditions of imperialism. • Define terms and concepts of social Darwinism, patriarchy, and capitalism. • Identify types and sources of power: political, economic, religious, and ideological.	Using case study material for 19th century Western, Middle Eastern, African, and Asian nations, build a graphic organizer that: • Identifies which nations had power and what type • Explains on what that power was built and exists • Explains how that power was exercised • Determines what impact the power of other nations had on each nation • Describes what conditions existed in each nation that resulted in becoming either a dominant or dominated nation	• Develop a white paper on the best solution for the United States and Allied forces to employ to ensure the safety and security of the people around the world by defeating groups such as ISIS. • Present three actions the United States and Allied nations can take to mitigate risk to citizens while building positive relations with previously imperialized regions of the world.

Source: Adapted from McDowell, 2017, pp. 61–62.

Identifying the project-design steps that are needed to ensure students are clear on the learning intentions and success criteria of project-based learning is a valuable action for teachers (and students) in the evidence-gathering phase. These projects begin in the classroom with students at the transfer level, making it critical that students have the support necessary to meet this expectation. To get to this level of the work, it is imperative that students have a balance of surface, deep, and transfer levels of knowledge and skill. As McDowell (2017) suggests, "This level of clarity of expectations will enable students to better progress toward established goals and address a multitude of problems outside the one offered in the class by the teacher, which is the ultimate goal of transfer" (p. 68).

Concluding Thoughts to Heighten Systems Thinking

This chapter has introduced you to the main aspects of gathering evidence as we build an Unstoppable Assessment system. If educators are going to take time away from their instruction to collaborate, the information gathered from their assessments should provide meaningful insight into what students do or do not know and to what level they know it. Educators also need to know if their instructional design and the teaching strategies they employ produce the desired levels of student performance.

Now that you and your teammates have had a chance to reflect on your current reality and consider the manner in which this work will strengthen your learning system as a whole, we invite you to take the next step toward maximizing your collaborative work and advancing your team's growth. Refer to the reproducible "Gathering Evidence Systems Protocol" (pages 76–77), and complete the protocol as a team *prior* to reading the next chapter. As you reflect on what this chapter affirmed, what you learned, and what may have given you pause, also use the reproducible template "Focusing Our View Within the System: Gathering Evidence" (page 78) to acknowledge your thoughts before moving forward.

Gathering Evidence Systems Protocol

Team Members: _____ Date: _____

Unit or Topic of Study: _____

Zoom In	*How will I determine if my students are making adequate progress toward the desired results?*	
	What is the expected level of performance at this point in the lesson/unit?	
Zoom Out	*How will we collect and organize our student work in order to effectively represent what our students know and can do as well as what they haven't learned just yet?*	

Collecting Evidence: Determine the task or learning activity that will be used to determine what students know and can do.

Tool Used	People Responsible	By When

Managing Evidence: Determine the common scoring criteria—a guide, checklist, or rubric—that will allow teachers to consistently monitor student learning and ensure all students are being measured to the same standard of performance.

Tool Used	People Responsible	By When

Organizing Evidence: Determine how to organize students' evidence so it is easily accessible by all members of the team.

Tool Used	People Responsible	By When

Assessing Unstoppable Learning © 2018 Solution Tree Press • SolutionTree.com
Visit **go.SolutionTree.com/assessment** to download this free reproducible.

Panoramic	*How will we prepare to report our evidence in order to efficiently discuss it with our colleagues and our students?*		
	Reporting Evidence: Determine how evidence will be viewed, interpreted, and represented prior to the next team meeting.		
	Expectations for teacher to record student data	Expectations for teacher to individually interpret their own students' data	Expectations for teacher to represent student needs and concerns

Focusing Our View Within the System: Gathering Evidence

Zoom In	Zoom Out
What is our current reality? What kind of information are we looking for to move us toward the results we desire?	Why do we need this information? How will it advance our work?
Panoramic	**View From Above**
How will these decisions or conversations impact our system? What is the potential to create greater balance and alignment within?	How will we leverage the gifts and talents of the people within the system to heighten systems thinking throughout?

CHAPTER 4

DISCUSSING EVIDENCE TO LEVERAGE ASSESSMENT AS LEARNING

Schools will not know whether or not all students are learning unless educators are hungry for evidence that students are acquiring the knowledge, skills, and dispositions deemed most essential to their success.

—Richard DuFour, Rebecca DuFour, and Robert Eaker

In chapter 1, we acknowledged the potential for fear to play a role in educators' ability to engage in meaningful, enriching collaborative work. When it comes to discussing evidence and data analysis, that fear has an opportunity to once again rise to the surface. Although educators have clearly stated what they want students to know and be able to do and at what level they want them to do it (and also determined the most appropriate methods and tasks to enable students to best demonstrate what they can do with what educators have taught), fear of what the evidence will reveal becomes a real concern for many teachers and teams. As they prepare for those collaborative conversations with colleagues, stomachs may turn as they consider the potential outcomes and reflect on their individual contributions to the overall success of the team.

In the quest to do right by students, teachers strive to achieve the highest levels of instructional performance so that students can achieve at the highest levels of performance. Yet the anxiety that a data conversation can cause for some team members could have such an impact that it actually hinders the conversation from ever happening in the first place. Schmoker (1999) offers the idea that educators avoid discussing data because they have great concern for data's "capacity to reveal strengths and weakness, failure and success" (p. 39). He states, "Education seems to maintain a tacit bargain among constituents at every level not to gather or use information that will reveal a clear need for improvement: where we need to do better, where we need to make changes" (p. 39).

The strength of the relationships on your team and the trust you have in each other will impact that very first data conversation you have. Even the strongest teams will struggle. In order to build a collective understanding of students' current level of performance, teachers must leverage those relationships to separate individual emotions from the team's focus on the results of its professional practice. When teams use this evidence to reveal what students have done as a result of instruction, teachers can better determine their collective effectiveness and begin to evaluate individual performance relative to the team's success. We are steeled by this assertion from Allan Odden and Sarah Archibald (2009):

> In schools that double student performance, teachers use results from common unit and interim assessments to help members of collaborative teams compare strategies and adopt those that are most effective. Instructional practice is out in the open, the subject of public and professional conversation, and the source of ongoing, job-embedded professional development. (as cited in DuFour et al., 2010, p. 187)

However, discussing evidence of student learning isn't as simple as one team member stating, "OK, everyone, let's sit down and look at some data!" We have brought intention and strategy to each tenet of the Unstoppable Assessment framework thus far. We will approach discussing evidence no differently. Parry Graham and William Ferriter (2010), Bruce Wellman and Laura Lipton (2004), Cassandra Erkens (2016), and Kim Bailey and Chris Jakicic (2012), among others, have introduced structured data conversation protocols to help teams remove emotion from the discussion and enable a genuine focus on what the information tells them about what students are learning. In this chapter, we provide protocols that are both a blend of our colleagues' existing protocols and our intentional efforts to promote healthy data conversations that advance systems thinking and student learning throughout the organization. After describing these protocols to illustrate the flow of conversation and articulate how each task interplays with another, we examine the role of causality conversations that help teams further discuss why the data reveal what they do and provide a template to guide these team conversations.

Before delving into the content, we want to emphasize two fundamental concepts that are important to keep in mind as you consider these methods for data discussion and begin team conversations:

1. We must always remember that there are faces—both student *and* adult—behind the numbers and data that educators discuss.

2. *Which* data educators talk about has far less significance in building trust and fostering healthy collaborative relationships than *how* they discuss data and *why* they discuss them.

Given that there are faces behind the numbers, building trust and fostering healthy relationships among teams is far from optional. Trusting, healthy teams have the courage to discuss results in a way that moves them to action.

> • **Zoom in:** Which student groups did we move to mastery? Which student groups do we still need to move to mastery? Do our results match our predictions for student performance?
>
> • **Zoom out:** How will we organize our corrective instruction for those students who continue to demonstrate difficulty? How will we organize our instruction for those students who are ready to advance beyond mastery? Which member or members of the team are best suited to provide those types of instruction?
>
> • **Panoramic:** What additional information or resources do we need now as a result of our evidence-based discussion? What is our next step as a result of our learning during our evidence-based discussion?

Protocols for Discussing Evidence

The three protocols in this chapter are suitable for different types of discussions around the evidence a team has gathered. The first protocol is most useful for discussing evidence from a common summative assessment, given at the end of a unit of study. The second and third protocols are more helpful when evaluating common formative assessments that teams may administer during the learning process.

Protocol 1: Evidence Systems Discussion

Teams can use this protocol for both designing common summative assessments and discussing the student evidence they gather after presenting a unit of study. Teams could also use this protocol for data review with state or provincial assessments, despite the absence of student work sampling. Angie uses this process with her leadership teams, including a group of more than one hundred learning leaders—district staff, principals, and systems thinking building staff—who use this protocol to glean information from their state standardized test results. The protocol consists of five sequential tasks that teams complete.

Task 1: Prediscussion Work

Teams preparing to discuss evidence will want to honor the intentional planning and preparation that have created this opportunity to reflect on student performance.

That said, the data can often initially raise more questions than they provide answers for. As such, as prediscussion work, each team member commits to reviewing his or her individual and collective team data prior to the meeting in order to best prepare to share both his or her *observations* and *questions* during the team discussion. As team members do their prediscussion homework, it's helpful to consider the following prompts for observations and questions while reviewing the data.

- The key considerations for observations are:
  - Are there patterns or trends in student performance? For example, did many students do well on certain learning targets or demonstrate difficulty with others?
  - How are various student groups performing in my classroom? Is that similar or different to their performance across the grade level?

- The key considerations for questions are:
  - Do our current pacing calendar and units of study support all students to reach proficiency?
  - Do we provide ample opportunity to check for understanding of learning before and during our instructional delivery?
  - Why have we been effective with some learners but not as effective with other student groups?

Before entering a data conversation, members strategically reflect on what they notice and what they are wondering. This reflection enables them to avoid making any assumptions about what the data might reveal. This helps everyone begin to replace those assumptions with focused questions to answer during the team data conversation. A tip to consider when completing task 1 is to use index cards or sticky notes, and write one observation or question per card or note. This will make it easier to cluster common ideas together in task 3.

Task 2: Data Organization

In the second task for this protocol, the work shifts from individual thought to collective discussion. Teachers have intentionally prepared this assessment or task in order to discuss more than whether students got the answers right or wrong. The team has designed the assessment so that it represents the most essential content and students have an opportunity to demonstrate their level of understanding on each of those learning progressions. Teams can clearly see which students perform at which level and how students demonstrate their thinking around what they learn.

Now comes the fun part! It's time to analyze the data. This portion of the protocol is more procedural—and more public—than the first task. Teams work collaboratively to document how students performed on each of the respective learning targets the assessment measured. Frequently, these data reviews entail looking at the points or marks students have received and attempting to ascertain patterns or trends in student performance. Teachers can collaboratively calculate their students' collective performance and can quickly see how many students have met the expected level of performance, how many approach that level of performance, and how many really struggle to demonstrate an understanding of the monitored skills and concepts. Data spreadsheets that use conditional formatting or other highlighting or annotation can further enhance this type of data review so the data analysis visually appeals to teams. Teams can more easily recognize and document the various levels of student performance based on the criteria they determined using such visualization tools.

Some teams choose to enter their data into a common data spreadsheet prior to the meeting for ease of organization and display. No matter your team's preference, we strongly advocate for calculating both the percentage and the actual number of students who performed at each level. Depending on how many students the group includes, a percentage could quickly misrepresent the amount of corrective instruction needed or, on the other hand, inflate the level of proficiency satisfied via this assessment of learning. This practice becomes even more valuable when looking at levels of learning by student demographics, such as gender or race. Knowing exactly how many student faces those data represent—and not just a percentage—keeps the focus right where it should be.

Teams can use the template provided in figure 4.1 (page 84) to insert the learning goals measured and label the criteria that they have established. For example, words like *proficient, approaching*, and *beginning* could serve as criteria to describe the level of learning evidenced from the student work. Note that, depending on the number of learning goals you examine, your team may not use all rows of the template, or you may need to add more rows.

Gleaning patterns and trends from student evidence plays a key part in the discussing evidence tenet of Unstoppable Assessment. Now we ask you to kick that practice up a notch. We want to make sure that, as you review your data, you also bring valid examples of student work to the table. Many teams we work with have dynamic and passionate conversations about what students know and what they do not know, yet the conversations lack actual pieces of student work. We believe this to be a significant (but easily remedied!) oversight, and addressing it would greatly enhance teams' ability to disaggregate the data by student group and more directly determine how their teaching impacts student performance for each type of learner. Using the actual student work also allows teachers to complete a more thorough error analysis to identify any misconceptions and recognize patterns in student thinking.

Task 3: Review and Prioritization

Teams now take time to reflect as individuals on the student evidence and collaboratively organize the data in order to highlight patterns and trends regarding how students demonstrated their learning. At this point in the protocol, we invite each

Learning Goal	Criteria:		Criteria:		Criteria:		Criteria:	
	Percentage	Number	Percentage	Number	Percentage	Number	Percentage	Number

Figure 4.1: Discussing evidence systems protocol—Task 2 considerations.

Visit go.SolutionTree.com/assessment to download a free reproducible version of this figure.

team member to look back at the observations and questions prepared during task 1 and spend a few minutes individually reviewing those initial thoughts and making any needed additions or modifications. During this independent reflection, use index cards or sticky notes to rewrite a few of your observations and a few questions you had from task 1 of your data review. This process brings each team member's voice to the conversation. It also honors collective thinking as the team clusters individual ideas together to bring clarity to common themes and common questions.

Once a team clusters together similar themes and questions, team members can recognize commonalities in their thinking. Teachers can now begin the process of making narrative statements to represent their common ideas. However, when it comes to systems thinking, we have to be critical consumers of the information we evaluate and the patterns and trends we realize in data. Not all statements are created equal, and this step in the protocol enables the team to assign a level of priority and a level of satisfaction to its observations and questions. For priority levels, the team uses a scale from 1 to 4, where 1 = highly unimportant, 2 = unimportant, 3 = important, and 4 = highly important. The scale for satisfaction levels is similar, as follows: 1 = highly dissatisfied, 2 = dissatisfied, 3 = satisfied, and 4 = highly satisfied. We suggest using a four-point scale in order to avoid defaulting to the middle by using a scale with an odd number of criteria points.

For example, a team may generate, based on a common observation, a narrative statement such as, "Forty-five percent of all eighth-grade females are proficient as compared to 86 percent of eighth-grade males." The team members discuss this statement and agree that they do not feel satisfied with this observation about their students' performance. They assign it a 1 relative to their level of satisfaction. They also believe this gender gap has great significance to their team, so they assign the level of importance a 4. A statement such as this, with low satisfaction and high importance, may emerge as a priority in the team's next instructional steps and action planning. Another example narrative statement might be, "Mathematics proficiency among our students receiving special education services grew from 35 percent in 2015 to 75 percent in 2016, resulting in fifty more students achieving proficiency." These data highly satisfy the team because of the large growth these learners demonstrated, so they assign their level of satisfaction a 4. The team members also find significance in this observation, and they begin to think about what may have caused such high levels of growth and attainment. They assign a level 4 to the importance of this statement. Figure 4.2 (page 86) provides a tool for teams to record the levels of satisfaction and importance they assign to their collective narrative statements. When completing this template for task 3, write one narrative statement per line and use a one-sided document. This enables more tactile learners to cut the template into strips when they get to task 4.

Data being analyzed: _____

Fill in the statements, and circle the satisfaction and importance levels (1–4) your team assigns for each.

Scale

1 = highly dissatisfied; highly unimportant   3 = satisfied; important

2 = dissatisfied; unimportant   4 = highly satisfied; highly important

Individual Observations:

Satisfaction Level	Statement	Importance Level
1 2 3 4		1 2 3 4
1 2 3 4		1 2 3 4
1 2 3 4		1 2 3 4
1 2 3 4		1 2 3 4
1 2 3 4		1 2 3 4

Figure 4.2: Narrative statements template.

Visit **go.SolutionTree.com/assessment** *for a free reproducible version of this figure.*

Task 4: Categorization

Once your team has given weight to each of its narrative statements, you have revealed some points of pride as well as some opportunities for improvement. Continuing with our assertion that not all narrative statements have equal weight or value, we now invite teams to sort each statement into one of three categories regarding their next steps: (1) sustain, (2) monitor, or (3) improve.

Statements in the *sustain* category represent points of pride that teams should celebrate and replicate. Students should continue to attain this level of success. Statements in the *monitor* category represent areas of team focus, team goals, or components that the team has collaboratively discussed and actively seeks new learning on. With some simple adjustments to instructional delivery, alignment of learning activities with assessment tasks, or utilization of a different curricular resource, teams could achieve even better results. Statements in the *improve* category indicate areas where learning and achievement have not yet reached the levels the team needs them to reach. These statements suggest more than a tweak and will likely require teachers to do things differently with their assessments or instructional delivery model in order to realize the desired results. Figure 4.3 provides a template for teams to sort their statements by category.

Category	Statements
Sustain: These statements represent points of pride that we should celebrate and replicate.	
Monitor: These statements represent something we have worked hard on, and with a tweak or two, we could amplify our instruction to achieve even better results.	
Improve: These statements represent data that aren't quite where we want them to be just yet. We need to do some things differently in order to interrupt this trend and improve student learning.	

Figure 4.3: Template for categorizing narrative statements.

*Visit **go.SolutionTree.com/assessment** for a free reproducible version of this figure.*

After categorizing their statements, teams should focus on the improvement areas they identified. Specifically, teams should examine how the questions they identified earlier align with what have emerged as priorities, and they should identify any additional questions they now have and what information they need to move forward. Later in this chapter, we will introduce a causality template that will better equip your team to ask provocative questions and make decisions about next steps.

Task 5: Reflection and Transparency

The final task of our protocol focuses on reflection and transparency as teams move forward. This final step challenges teams to promote transparency in their future collaboration and implementation of effective practices in order to collectively ensure each student's mastery of the essential learning. Teams should discuss and record their responses to the questions in figure 4.4.

Question	Response
Which student groups did we move to mastery? Which student groups do we still need to move to mastery?	
How will we organize our corrective instruction for those students who continue to demonstrate difficulty? Which member or members of the team are best suited to provide that instruction?	
How will we organize our instruction for those students who are ready to advance beyond mastery? Which member or members of the team are best suited to provide that instruction?	
What additional information or resources do we need now as a result of our evidence-based discussion?	
What is our next step as a result of our learning during our evidence-based discussion?	

Figure 4.4: Discussing evidence systems protocol—Task 5 considerations.

*Visit **go.SolutionTree.com/assessment** for a free reproducible version of this figure.*

Taking time for everyone to reflect individually during prediscussion work can really set the stage for robust conversations throughout the subsequent tasks in this protocol and ensure that all voices have an equal opportunity to contribute to the dialogue. The strength of your team's relationships and the trust you have in each other will impact each data conversation you have. Remember, even the strongest teams will struggle. In order to build a collective understanding of their students' current level of performance, teachers must leverage those relationships and separate individual emotions from the team's focus on the results of their professional practice. When teachers use their evidence to reveal what their students have done as a result of their instruction, they can better determine their collective effectiveness and begin to evaluate their individual performance relative to their team's success. As you work through this protocol with your team, use the "Discussing Evidence Systems Protocol Guide" reproducible at **go.SolutionTree.com/assessment** to guide your conversations and analysis of student evidence.

Protocol 2: Team Learning Log

Mike Schmoker (2011) introduced the concept of a team learning log (TLL), which invites teams through an efficiently structured data meeting cycle. The team learning log asks teachers to identify a targeted standard or area of weakness, design a common assessment to evaluate what students know and can do, and then determine the instructional strategy or strategies that will best enable all students to reach the desired level of mastery. This process can be part of a one- to four-week cycle, and teams revisit it after they give an assessment so they can document results and make any necessary adjustments to instruction.

Figure 4.5 offers an example of a learning log used by a third-grade team we worked with. This log allowed the team to align their work more precisely to the kinds of conversations it had in its weekly team meetings. Teams use this protocol for common formative assessments to discuss the student evidence gathered either during or after a unit of study.

This team found value in revisiting its previously targeted skill and making sure that students still performed on track. This approach also gave team members a great way to celebrate their students' collective success and determine any further needs for individual students. They documented individual students, by their initials, on a separate electronic tracking document to most effectively monitor students' initial performance alongside their respective growth throughout the course of instruction. The team also identified which corrective instruction or intervention to provide to each student. This step was an essential part of this team's work to guarantee that each student would achieve mastery. The team members' discussion and documentation of their work with students enabled them to sustain the practices that worked and strategically abandon pieces that did not yield the desired results. (We will further discuss how teams respond to evidence in chapter 5.)

Team Learning Log for Grade 3:
Minnesota Comprehensive Assessment (MCA) Measurement Strand

Date: February 21, 2008

Targeted standard or area of weakness (the area of weakness should be identified from a state-, district-, or grade-level common assessment)
Currently, more than 50 percent of our third-grade students lack proficiency in each of the five strands of measurement conversion and comparison on MCA math practice test #1.

Goal (the goal must be: strategic and specific, measurable, attainable, results oriented, and time bound)
One hundred percent of third-grade students will demonstrate proficiency in the area of measurement conversion and comparison by February 29, 2008.

Instructional solution (should include a brief description of the lesson plan or intervention strategy)

Students will be divided into six groups during our math intervention time of 11:00–11:30. Kristin, Wendy, Angie, Catherine, Jan, Kim, and Sheila will lead groups. Sheila will see students who are in other classes during that time period during a "lunch bunch" group from 12:05–12:25.

Note: Instructional strategies used will reflect the same format and questioning style used on the MCAs. Each teacher will deliver instruction during the week of February 25–29. Each teacher will cover the same concepts and outline for each lesson given.

Each classroom will be divided into stations. Students will complete independent, targeted MCA prep work (weekly packets) while they wait to cycle through the following schedule.

Day 1: Small group (3–6 students) direct instruction with teacher to clarify key measurement vocabulary

- Catherine will prepare a list of vocabulary for each teacher according to current MCA-II test specifications.

Day 2: Partner work with teacher to sort measurement words by category (such as length, weight, and volume)

- Kristin will prepare two vocabulary sort activities for guided practice.

Days 3 and 4: Guided or independent practice with teacher using worksheets from various resources (mailbox, teacher files, and Montessori packets)

- Wendy will prepare 1–2 pages of pencil-and-paper practice for days 3 and 4.
- Day 3: All groups will have guided pencil-and-paper practice.
- Day 4: On-level and advanced students will complete independent practice. Below-level students will regroup to review vocabulary and key measurement concepts based on need.

Common assessment (to be used to evaluate instructional solution; assessments must be formative and common to all grade-level team members)
We will determine effectiveness of our strategy through a four-point assessment, to be given the afternoon of February 29th. The assessment directions will be scripted to ensure consistent delivery for accurate results. Angie will prepare this assessment.

Figure 4.5: Team learning log.

continued →

Results (measurable impact of solution; this portion can only be filled out *after* the common assessment has been given; the assessment should occur 3–6 weeks after the instructional solution begins)

Here are the results that show growth from our initial evaluation to our assessment. The results are disaggregated by each specific measurement strand.

Best unit of measurement (length):

- MCA Practice Test – 38 not passing
- TLL Assessment – **15** not passing

Best unit of measurement (weight):

- MCA Practice Test – 34 not passing
- TLL Assessment – **15** not passing

Best tool for measurement:

- MCA Practice Test – 41 not passing
- TLL Assessment – **6** not passing

Volume:

- MCA Practice Test – no tested question
- TLL Assessment – **18** not passing

Constructed Response (no common specific instruction):

- MCA Practice Test – about 60 points missed
- TLL Assessment – about 46 points missed

Fifteen students did not pass our **total** assessment.

Next steps (outline the instructional adjustments needed; based on results, identify the next steps to address any continuing areas of concern or to identify a new goal)

The fifteen students who did not pass were placed into intervention groups with Jan and Sheila. Students who did not pass were identified as those who scored less than +3/4 on the assessment. We are continuing to develop a plan for next steps with the concepts of measurement (for example, conversions such as 100 cm = 1m).

Administrator feedback

Targeted standard or area of weakness:

Instructional solution:

Common assessment:

Results:

Next step:

The team then tackled a new skill or benchmark and mapped out the instructional solutions and strategies. The team revisited this learning log once it had completed the instructional cycle, documented its results, and determined next steps for students who had not yet met the benchmark. For the most essential skills, active monitoring, intentional planning, and timely discussion of student evidence yield incredible student growth and guarantee students' readiness for the next level of learning.

Protocol 3: Pile, Stack, and Plan

This protocol for organizing student work comes from Vagle (2015). Teams use this protocol to review and discuss the student evidence they have gathered from common formative assessments and develop instructional plans for students who have mastered the skill and are ready for extension, students who are almost there but need a bit more practice, and students who need additional time and support to learn the material. Although teams should be able to complete the entire process in a typical team meeting (thirty to forty minutes), Vagle (2015) offers that—like with anything else—the first time or two may extend beyond one meeting as teams learn and practice a new way of discussing student evidence. Vagle (2015) outlines the first five steps of the process as follows:

1. Choose one essential learning goal.

2. Create a short common assessment to check understanding.

3. Bring student work to your team meeting to review, identify strengths and misconceptions, and come to consensus on next steps for improvement.

4. Sort student work in piles based on common mistakes and areas of need.

5. Plan instruction for each of those groups.

Vagle suggests that teams use figure 4.6 to focus their work.

Learning Goal or Misconception to Work On:	Learning Goal or Misconception to Work On:	Learning Goal or Misconception to Work On:
Students:	Students:	Students:
Instructional Plan: 1. 2. 3.	Instructional Plan: 1. 2. 3.	Instructional Plan: 1. 2. 3.

Source: Adapted from Chapman & Vagle, 2011.

Figure 4.6: Instructional response planning form.

Teams then close this process with reflective questions and key planning considerations moving forward, such as:

- How timely will will our response be to the information learned from the assessment? When will the response occur during the school day?

- How will we monitor the effectiveness of the instructional response?

- How will we embed student self-reflection as part of our instructional response and future lesson planning?

Causality Conversations

No matter which level of data analysis and review occurs in a team, as teachers reflect on the observations, questions, and priorities that have emerged from their evidence-based discussions, it becomes difficult to temper the sense of urgency the conclusions present. It is natural for teachers to identify a problem and immediately want to work toward resolving it. However, often the data they discuss do not answer *why* the results are the way they are. Whether the data reveal opportunities to celebrate the work of a team or opportunities to continue making adjustments and improvements, teams further enhance systems thinking when they engage in causality conversations that help answer the *why*. Answering the *why* promotes a focus on continuous improvement and sustainability of efforts.

Figure 4.7 provides a template to help guide teams through a causality conversation. Teams identify one of their opportunities for improvement as a *student learning concern*. Teachers then engage in dialogue around the types of systemic support that curriculum, assessment, and instruction provide to students. Further, teams discuss the impact that student engagement and the overall structures and systems within the building may have on student achievement. The key questions indicated in the template are intended to provide teams with a place to start for the areas of curriculum, assessment, instruction, student engagement, and structures and systems. Your team may generate new questions or have concerns that have more pertinence to your team or building and are not represented here. The key idea here is that your team engages in conversation around *why* you get the results you do.

Concluding Thoughts to Heighten Systems Thinking

This chapter has introduced aspects of discussing evidence as we build an Unstoppable Assessment system. Now that you and your teammates have had a chance to reflect on your current reality and consider the manner in which this work will strengthen your learning system as a whole, we invite you to take the next step by trying out one of the protocols introduced in this chapter—or by beginning to tackle the causality conversation—in order to maximize your collaborative work and advance your team's growth *prior* to reading the next chapter. As you reflect on what this chapter affirmed, what you learned, and what may have given you pause, use the reproducible template "Focusing Our View Within the System: Discussing Evidence" (page 94) to acknowledge your thoughts before moving forward.

Student Learning Concern:					
	Curriculum	**Assessment**	**Instruction**	**Student Engagement**	**Structures and Systems**
Key Questions	To what extent do the current pacing calendar and units of study support all students reaching proficiency? Are all team members implementing the curriculum with the same level of fidelity?	To what extent do we check for understanding of student learning before, during, and after instruction? What are the data telling us about our effectiveness with each learner?	To what extent do we have evidence on the effectiveness of our instructional practices? How well are we connecting with each learner in our classroom?	To what extent are students active participants in the learning process? Is instruction done *to* them or *for* them? To what level do students feel welcome and supported in their classrooms?	To what extent does the master schedule support equitable opportunities for students to learn the content? To what level are teachers engaged in collaborative team conversations to support their own individual growth and development?
Possible Causes					
Our Level of Control (Total, Partial, or None)					
Actions for Growth					
Key People and Resources Needed					

Figure 4.7: Causality conversation template.

*Visit **go.SolutionTree.com/assessment** for a free reproducible version of this figure.*

Focusing Our View Within the System:
Discussing Evidence

Zoom In	Zoom Out
What is our current reality? What kind of information are we looking for to move us toward the results we desire?	Why do we need this information? How will it advance our work?
Panoramic	**View From Above**
How will these decisions or conversations impact our system? What is the potential to create greater balance and alignment within?	How will we leverage the gifts and talents of the people within the system to heighten systems thinking throughout?

CHAPTER 5

RESPONDING TO EVIDENCE TO ADAPT ASSESSMENT AS INSTRUCTION

Our self- or team reflection on our work as adults will give us great insight into the effectiveness of our efforts and mobilize us for next steps to ensure high levels of learning for every student. It's our intentions not their variables that will provide the key to unlocking their potential.

—Tom Hierck

This chapter furthers the previously discussed concepts of collaborating and seeking, gathering, and discussing evidence by examining how to guide the response to the evidence. A first step is to reflect on what we, as teachers, have done to ensure that our students become proficient in the essential learning or prioritized content. As we discuss the evidence we have sought and gathered from our students, their performance reveals how well our instruction resulted in the levels of learning we desire. Reflecting on past instructional practice helps educators gain insight into which instructional strategies were most successful and what they can do to strengthen future practice. Additionally, reflecting and responding as a team deprivatizes the work of educators and strengthens the culture of a professional learning community.

The time spent in collaboration provides teachers the opportunity to deepen understanding of course content, review successful and not-so-successful strategies, improve interactions with students and colleagues, develop a capacity to embrace differences and differentiate (including adapting, modifying, and making accommodations) for those differences, and work toward a more collaborative approach to teaching and learning as part of a larger, interdependent team. The response to the question, What else can I do to ensure proficiency? needs to drive all this work. The more educators gather to discuss the evidence of students' progress toward mastery, the richer the conversations become. These discussions focus collaborative conversations around student achievement and yield greater potential for generating solutions to the not-yet-mastered scenarios with students. Educators can then respond to the evidence (achievement data) that reflects areas of need by adapting instruction.

In this chapter, we will focus on some important aspects that support responding to evidence, including data team processes, differentiation, reciprocity of assessment and instruction, response to instruction and intervention planning, teacher capacity, student investment, and goal reflection.

> - **Zoom in:** Based on your current level of assessment literacy, how do you use evidence gained from assessment to adjust your instructional design?
> - **Zoom out:** How will our collaborative team processes and learning drive how each student receives the instruction he or she needs as he or she needs it?
> - **Panoramic:** How does the manner in which we seek, gather, and discuss evidence enable us to accurately respond to that evidence?

Data Team Processes

Douglas Reeves (2010) coined the term *data team* to describe the process by which educators make data-driven decisions at the classroom level. These teams follow a specific step-by-step process to examine student work, apply effective instructional strategies and interventions, and monitor student learning in response to supplemental interventions. Here are the five steps in the process.

1. **Collect and chart the data:** Teams gather and disaggregate data from common formative assessments.

2. **Analyze data and prioritize needs:** Teams identify the strengths and needs of students and prioritize the most urgent needs based on inferences drawn from the data.

3. **Establish SMART (strategic and specific, measurable, attainable, results-oriented, and time-bound) goals:** Teams that engage in the SMART goal process regularly review and revise these goals through their data team work.

4. **Select instructional strategies:** Analyses of the data help guide educators in selecting the most appropriate strategies to use when intervening with students who have not yet attained proficiency.

5. **Determine results indicators:** Educators determine what measures will indicate that they have succeeded. They monitor the selected strategies for their impact. If student results do not show improvement, educators discuss and implement midcourse corrections.

As the process starts over at step one at the team's next meeting, the team must remember the work is in constant flux. Throughout the cycle, teams monitor and evaluate progress to determine whether goals have been met. Collectively, educators possess the expertise to meet all students' needs. Through the various analyses, teams can plan the next steps, including any additional supports that some students will need. Questions such as the following should guide the planning.

- What interventions will we provide?

- When will we provide these interventions?

- Who will provide these interventions?

- What strategies, resources, and staff will we use in these interventions?

- How will we monitor student progress to measure the effectiveness of these interventions?

See figure 5.1 for an example of what a data team in action might look and sound like. This example highlights the elements of effective collaboration, a focus on results, the expectation that all students will attain proficiency, and the acceptance that for this to occur, it rests with the adults.

The fifth-grade mathematics team gathers to talk about the results of the pretest it just administered on the topic of adding and subtracting fractions with like and unlike denominators. The results show that 30 percent of the students achieved *proficient* scores, with the rest of the class scoring at the *far from proficient* level. One of the team members had taken responsibility for collecting and charting the data, and it is available for all to see at the start of the meeting. The team members then engage in dialogue about what they see as strengths and challenges for the students. They agree that students are able to add and subtract fractions with like denominators and appear to be fluent in finding the least common multiple. The data also lead them to believe that their teaching should focus on the need to identify a common denominator when adding or subtracting fractions

---

Figure 5.1: A fishbowl view of data team dialogue. continued →

and on converting fractions once the common denominator has been achieved. The team establishes a SMART goal for the unit and has determined that "the percentage of students scoring at the proficient level and higher on the fraction addition/subtraction postassessment will increase from the 30 percent who did so on the pretest to 80 percent, as measured by the teacher-made fraction addition and subtraction postassessment." The discussion shifts to instructional strategies, and the team agrees to provide extension work for students who have mastered the skill and spends extra time providing direct instruction and extra practice for students who are not proficient. Some suggestions they have at this stage include:

- Have students play a fraction addition and subtraction game online.
- Review the introductory minilesson with small groups.
- Teach the minilesson and complete a practice sheet on finding common denominators.
- Set up peer-to-peer grouping where the proficient students work with those approaching proficiency, while the teacher works with the students most in need.

As the meeting time concludes, the team establishes what it will use as results indicators. Team members expect that the postassessment results will be significantly higher than the pretest results, as noted previously. Beyond that, they also want to observe their students conceptually representing adding fractions using visual models, to observe students going through each of the steps to add and subtract fractions, and to ensure that they are engaged in each of the learning experiences that are built into the unit.

Source: Adapted from Hierck & Weber, 2014, pp. 77–78.

Teachers' capacity will improve because of the collaborative learning opportunities that data teams promote. Finding moments to collectively respond to evidence will ensure that the evidence drives the teaching and learning cycle.

Differentiation

Collaborative teams respond to evidence by differentiating their next steps to ensure all students receive the subsequent layer of instruction in a way that activates their learning. Teams maximize differentiation when they use information from assessment data analysis to plan for it. Carol Ann Tomlinson (2014) reminds us that we can differentiate based on content, process, product, or environment. In this vein, teams can utilize the causality conversation activity introduced in chapter 4 (see figure 4.7, page 93) in order to determine what is currently preventing students from achieving mastery and then plan accordingly for each student's individual needs. Fisher and Frey (2015) share the notion that students are diverse in a variety of ways, including the following.

- **Knowledge:** All students have prior knowledge—some of it fully accurate, and some of it partially so. Graham Nuthall (2007) suggests that students already know on average about 50 percent of what a teacher intends for them to learn, although that 50 percent is not evenly distributed. Some students may have more topic knowledge than others. Teachers need to meet students at their level and move them to proficiency and beyond.

- **Readiness and abilities:** Teachers match instructional strategies to the abilities of their students, thereby ensuring a stretch for those who need it, a deepening for those on track who need practice, and scaffolding for those striving for proficiency.

- **Background:** The year 2014 marked the first year that nonwhite students made up the majority of the U.S. student population (Hussar & Bailey, 2014). This provides a richness of cultures and viewpoints in schools, and differentiating allows for all these viewpoints to be expressed.

- **Language:** An outgrowth of the previous point is that schools also see a wider array of languages that students speak. While language fluency occurs, differentiation allows for other learning to take place as well.

- **Interests:** Wherever practical and possible (and as educators strive to heighten engagement), educators should consider student interests in a differentiated classroom and incorporate those topics into instruction.

Teachers may misapply differentiation if they liken it to lowering the bar so all students succeed. Dylan Wiliam and Siobhan Leahy (2015) suggest that all students should have similar goals and that "differentiation should take place in terms of success criteria rather than the learning intentions" (p. 36). Collaborative teams can determine both what and how to differentiate by referencing the performance expectations they have set for students and comparing those expectations to what evidence students actually produced. This process eliminates the "I taught it, but the kids just didn't learn it" conversation entirely. Having accurate information in real time and through short-cycle assessments allows for teachers to respond and close gaps. The evidence gathered through quality assessment is the engine that drives success. The accuracy of that information enables teachers to productively respond to students' needs and close learning gaps. Teachers should not make decisions in the absence of evidence, and they should not view decisions made via evidence as *permanent* (labels forever attached to a student) but only as relevant until the next data set emerges to guide the next decisions. The grade 3 team we highlighted in the second protocol in chapter 4 (page 89) is masterful at this practice; no student is ever left behind because they are never done gathering and discussing evidence around the required levels of mastery.

Fisher and Frey (2015) identify several techniques for differentiation for before instruction, during instruction, and after instruction. As we consider how students learn—in the context of *what* we want students to learn—differentiating our approaches and our responses can move students toward mastery of skills and concepts in a more systematic manner. Consider the suggestions in table 5.1 (page 100) as you reflect on your students' needs in various moments of their learning.

Table 5.1: Techniques for Differentiating Instruction

Technique	Purpose
RAFT: Role, audience, format, and topic	Teachers can assign RAFT, an adaptable writing strategy, on a content-related topic but differentiate it for student readiness. Preteach the acronym so students will recognize this technique and learn to construct their own RAFTs. • **Role:** What is the student's role as the writer (for example, scientist, inventor, historian, reporter, or researcher)? • **Audience:** Who is the intended reader (for example, peers, teachers, animals or objects, parents, scientific community, or activists)? • **Format:** What's the best product (for example, journal, lab report, brochure, song, critique, or news article)? • **Topic:** What, who, or when is the subject (for example, an issue of personal or public interest or concern, a topic related to a question or problem, a historical time or figure, or a prediction for the future)?
Think-pair-share	Think-pair-share fosters higher-quality responses and encourages increased participation during classroom discussions by asking students to: • Think quietly about their answer • Pair with a peer to discuss ideas • Share their responses with the entire class All students are able to participate at their own readiness level, while each step provides a different pathway to meet multiple learning profiles.
Tiered instruction	Tiered instruction is a means of teaching one concept and meeting the different learning needs in a group. For example, a teacher provides some students with direct instruction on the types of simple machines and asks them to classify examples of each type. She provides other students with the more open-ended task of working in teams to describe the types of simple machines, then list and explain everyday examples of their own.
Word wall	New vocabulary words are posted in a prominent location and used as a student resource. Students use the word wall to help them recall key words when writing and speaking. Teachers can ask students to make connections between words to help them build their science vocabulary.
Vocabulary builders	Crossword puzzles, word searches, jumbles, and games like Pictionary and Scrabble all assist students in learning and using new vocabulary. Teachers can arrange vocabulary words into groups based on word families, complexity, or importance to key concepts, then students can work in groups based on their prior knowledge, readiness, and learning profiles.
Learning centers	Learning centers provide groups of students an opportunity to interact with new content. Centers typically include books, activities, and other print and media resources about related topics, such as space exploration, famous astronauts, constellations, Mars, model making, the big bang, science fiction, and others.

Source: Fisher & Frey, 2015, p. 119.

As with any academic learning target, the key to all students becoming proficient in social behaviors (like cooperation, respect, and attentiveness) or academic behaviors (like metacognition, self-regulation, and motivation) is to have a plan to scaffold the learning and meet the needs of students at their current levels. Following are suggested differentiation strategies that may help you support targets for student behavior.

- **Modify the learning environment:** With a proactive approach (if we can predict it, we can prevent it), teachers identify and modify specific environmental variables that may contribute to problem behavior. Teachers have the classroom layout, agenda of activities, procedures and routines, and instructional strategies under their control.

- **Decrease student uncertainty:** One of the areas that presents a significant challenge for students not yet proficient in desired behavioral outcomes is noninstructional or transitional time. Teachers can prepare students for transitions by providing a warning about the close of one activity and the opening of another, giving clear and brief directions, planning for any materials needed and having them on hand, and immediately starting the next content piece.

- **Provide opportunities to make choices:** Student engagement increases and disruption decreases when teachers offer students choices. Consider the order or number of activities, the choice of materials to use, or the possibility of allowing students to work with a partner.

- **Identify positive ways for students to communicate:** An extension of giving students choices is to work with students on their ability to recognize when they reach the verge of demonstrating some negative behavior. This could involve students using color cards to indicate to the teacher when they need to change their setting, where red might signal a crisis or an agreed-on time-out area of the room.

- **Use a variety of instructional strategies and classroom locations:** Teachers should use a variety of instructional strategies and locations in the classroom to maximize student engagement. Placing high-interest activities after challenging learning targets (academic or behavioral) may serve as an incentive for students to work toward demonstrating proficiency.

- **Recognize positive behaviors:** When a student behaves appropriately, reinforce the behavior. At that moment, the teacher should acknowledge the student's growth. It is also very important that adults model the desired behavior. For example, if a student acts disrespectfully, the adult must respond respectfully to model the desired outcome. A teacher will not effectively teach a student about respect if he or she instead reverts to disrespecting the student.

Assessment and Instruction: Two Sides of the Same Coin

At times, it appears that assessment and instruction are the education equivalent of the chicken-and-egg analogy—which came first? In reality, these two concepts are two sides of the same coin. Assessment does not occur solely after instruction or even apart from instruction. It's not just a pencil-and-paper test, nor a device designed to rank and sort students. Effective assessment is embedded in the instructional process, and assessment and instruction can happen at the same time. When teachers clearly state the goals of a lesson, an impromptu student comment can serve as an opportunity for assessment and drive the next bit of instruction, as teachers respond to the learning in the moment by adapting instruction.

Teachers design formative assessments to assess the key learning outcomes of the priority standards or essential learning targets. Three criteria to make formative assessments beneficial and to produce positive outcomes are as follows.

1. If a student achieves a proficient score, that score must accurately indicate that a student has learned what was intended.

2. If a student achieves a "not yet" score, that score should clearly and specifically indicate that the student needs additional support.

3. When data teams analyze the data and look at the errors students made, the errors must help efficiently determine student needs and target intervention. Tom Hierck and Chris Weber (2014) suggest this can inform future practice by examining the following questions.

   • To what extent—and with what success—did the team guide all students toward mastery?

   • What concepts or skills need to be reviewed with the entire class?

   • What factors have contributed to student difficulties?

   • What additional strategies and resources does the team need to ensure students improve their mastery?

   • What patterns can the team identify from student errors?

   • Among data team members, which instructional strategies proved most effective?

   • Among data team members, which instructional strategies proved ineffective?

   • How can the team improve the assessment?

   • Which students need more time and an alternative approach?

- With which standards and skills do these students need more time and an alternative approach?

Assessment and instruction cannot occur in isolation or without driving each other; it's not an *or* decision but an *and* expectation.

Response to Instruction and Effective Intervention Planning

One of the most comprehensive and extensively researched practices to guide educators as they respond to evidence of student learning and to ensure all students become proficient in the essential learning or prioritized content is response to intervention (RTI). RTI is a three-tiered framework of high-quality instruction and interventions to address students' learning needs. Tier 1 includes regular classroom instruction of the core curriculum. Tier 2 provides supplemental interventions to students who perform slightly below grade level. Intensive interventions for students well below grade level are reserved for Tier 3 (Buffum, Mattos, & Weber, 2009). Within an RTI framework, teachers engage students in the rich, deep learning experiences of Tier 1 core instruction while providing the necessary, targeted interventions to close achievement gaps and accelerate learning. It's clear that some students will need more time and alternative approaches to reach proficiency. This is predictable. However, they do not need remedial instruction, removal from class, or watered-down expectations; they need Tier 2 support. Evidence-gathering tools (diagnostics, referrals, and so on) drive Tier 2 interventions. Tier 2 represents targeted interventions to help students master the desired outcomes not sufficiently learned during core instruction in Tier 1.

Educators should also provide intensive, individualized interventions for students with significant deficits (multiple years behind in foundational prerequisite skills like self-regulation, organization, empathy, and attentiveness). The goal of Tier 3 interventions is to accelerate learning through diagnostically driven support to close gaps, not to provide a separate but unequal (and often isolated) behavioral experience. Thus, RTI shifts a school's response to struggling learners from a remediation model that too often masks learning needs, to one of targeted interventions that promote accelerated learning and higher levels of achievement. A teacher's approach to RTI must allow for Tiers 1, 2, *and* 3.

Teacher Capacity

Although students experience a variety of circumstances that we, as teachers, have no control over or capacity to alter, we do have the capacity to impact teaching. As John Hattie (2003) states, "It is what teachers know, do, and care about which is very powerful in this learning equation" (p. 2). How teachers understand assessment within this equation and, more important, how teachers can improve their assessment literacy go a long way in also defining their misconceptions or misinterpretations of formative assessment. A lack of clarity may have adverse effects on their classroom practices, which, in turn, has the potential to lower student learning outcomes. In order to improve outcomes for all, collaborative teams need to intentionally focus on increasing assessment literacy for all members. The more educators in a department, school, or district can collaborate, the greater the potential for those improved student outcomes.

As PLCs establish a collective commitment to this work, they may require an examination of existing policies, procedures, or practices that educators need to let go of and those that educators need to add. They may also require a broader discussion of how they coordinate professional development in the department, school, or district. To educate all students to higher levels of learning around prioritized state, provincial, and district standards, teachers need time and support to enable them to respond to student performance with instructional agility and revise their instruction and assessment in a timely (for the student) fashion. Teachers' fluency and reflections on their classroom practices will lead to improvements, but only when done collaboratively with their colleagues in a positive learning environment driven by evidence of student learning.

Commitment to a professional learning community extends beyond having conversations about what works for students and how teachers can ensure that all students achieve the desired outcomes. Collaborative team conversations also need to deal with expanding the toolbox of every teacher through increasing teachers' knowledge, awareness, and literacy of effective assessment practices. The greater the capacity for teachers, the better the results for students.

Student Investment

Educators do not have sole responsibility for responding to assessment data. Students must also play an active role in reflecting and acting on the evidence. Vagle (2015) defines *student investment* as "the extent to which students are engaged in their learning and moving toward independence in describing where they are and how to grow" (p. 86). Student investment becomes high when we use assessment to build hope, efficacy, and empowerment. Vagle (2015) notes the following student outcomes in environments with high student investment. Students:

- Have language to describe their learning
- Have a clear idea of quality and not-so-quality work
- Take action on descriptive feedback
- Revise their work

- Self-reflect on what the assessment means in terms of their learning

- Set goals based on assessment information

- Make an action plan in partnership with teachers to achieve their goals and improve

- Share their work and plans to improve (p. 11)

High levels of student investment occur when we design assessment strategies to have students actively engage in revising their work and fixing their mistakes. This means viewing assessment not as an endpoint to learning but as an integral part of learning.

As part of a balanced approach, summative assessment can increase student investment by including opportunities for self-assessment and by having clarity on the meaning of the final results. When educators utilize assessment in this fashion, the classroom culture shifts to a focus on learning and the role assessment plays in supporting that learning. Students who know what targets they already have proficiency in, what targets they are close to proficiency in, and what targets represent their best growth opportunities see the value, relevance, and meaning in the work they do. In essence, they learn how to learn. They gain confidence in their own capacity as learners and do not solely depend on the teacher for feedback. They take risks and trust their own judgment as well as peers' judgment. They become increasingly self-reliant for their learning.

James Nottingham (2017) describes the concept of a *learning pit* that students may enter when a new concept challenges them or teachers ask them to provide more detail on a concept they believe they already know. It brings the concepts of *challenge* and *confidence building* back into the learning equation. Nottingham (2017) describes the pit as "a place that teaches students not to sit back and wait for the answer to fall into their lap; instead it requires them to think about almost every decision that they make." Table 5.2 outlines the four stages of the learning pit.

Table 5.2: Four Stages of the Learning Pit

Stage 1: Identify the Key Concept	Conceptual analysis helps students make meaning of the world. Students always enter the learning pit as a result of focusing on a key concept that is broad and general, such as democracy, culture, music, or reality TV.
Stage 2: Challenge	Students are challenged to think more creatively and critically, collaborate with others, and communicate their thinking. Students address the 4Cs of 21st century learning as they dig deeper. Allowing for challenge is also one of the three key attributes of expert teaching, according to Hattie's (2009) research.

continued →

| Stage 3: Construct | This is the stage where students construct and co-construct an understanding of the concepts through meaningful dialogue. |
| Stage 4: Reflect | Students reflect on the learning journey they just took, examining what worked well and what strategies merit further use. |

Source: Adapted from Nottingham, 2017.

Nottingham's evidence suggests that students who spend time in the pit achieve better grades and improve as learners. When students are in the pit, they are predisposed to think more about and focus intently on the problem. This also builds their confidence and self-esteem as they overcome the challenge.

Engaging students in self-reflection to honor their own strengths and next steps on an assessment promotes a similar sense of ownership and partnership in the learning process. Figure 5.2 features an example of a reflection sheet that students could use after an assessment. Figure 5.3 features an example of a reflection sheet teachers and students can use together, with teachers filling out the top portion and students filling out the bottom portion.

Assignment: _____

Name: _____ Date: _____

Assessment Item or Number	Your Answer	Correct Answer	✓ if Your Answer was Incorrect	Explain the Mistake	Fix It or Prove It

Source: © 2016 Scott Greseth, Maplewood Middle School, Maplewood, Minnesota. Adapted with permission.

Figure 5.2: Self-reflection sheet.

Student Assessment Reflection

Name: _____

Hour: _____ Date: _____

Learning Target or Concept	Item Numbers	Student Score

Error Analysis

Item Number	Learning Target	Simple Mistake?	Action Plan (daily assignment, review sheet, or Moodle)

Rate your confidence level by circling the phrase that best describes how you think you did.

| I am confident I understand. | I knew what to do but have some questions. | I was unsure about what to do. | I guessed. |

Source: © 2016 Pam Bloom, Stillwater Area High School, Stillwater, Minnesota. Adapted with permission.

Figure 5.3: Student assessment reflection sheet.

Goal Reflection

Reflection is a critical aspect of teachers' work. Goal reflection is about looking at an objective for the unit and seeing what worked and what didn't. Having high levels of success and not knowing what caused that makes it hard to replicate that success and may result in us attributing success to luck or a strong student cohort. Having low levels of success and not knowing what impacted that makes it hard to change practices and may result in excuse making. Involving students in this reflection process acts as an essential component to grow *their* ownership of their learning. Let's examine this through the lenses of status goals and growth goals.

Status Goals

We define *status* as the moment of proficiency, a student's progress relative to the threshold (the bar or better) or expectation that has been defined. Clarity is critical, as students need to know the expectations and how to reach them. Teachers don't always have control in defining the goal, as often the academic content (curriculum guides or standards), the state or province, or the school or district has defined proficiency while also identifying the rigor. Nevertheless, teachers have the capacity to ensure all students build strength and stamina. This may drive the need to accommodate or modify the outcomes based on students' needs and current level of readiness. Accommodation refers to support in one area, not the one we are measuring, whereas modification refers to support in the area we are measuring. An analogy that you might find helpful is that you would consider eyeglasses an accommodation for a driving test (allowing you to perform the required skills or answer the questions because you can see them clearly) but a modification for an eye examination (giving you an advantage in seeing the letters that make up the test). Status goals, in essence, certify whether a student has made it.

One challenge with status goals is that they often give an inaccurate picture of what students can do, particularly for those students who might have accelerated beyond the goal. If you set the bar too low, some may step over it without much effort. Tom already sees this with one of his granddaughters, who gets bored with her homework (a matter for a whole other book as far as the efficacy and impact of this practice in the primary grades!) after the first three questions and then rushes to complete the rest, resulting in concentration, not competency, errors. A second challenge with status goals occurs if a status goal is linked to an assessment students only take once. This leaves us asking the questions, "What does the result of the assessment indicate? Do we only offer one shot to get proficient? and Does the lack of achieved proficiency on the assessment change the notion of essential learning to helpful learning?" Although we agree that better assessments could give better feedback, we also stress that we must make the goal *proficiency*, not timeliness. This is why we suggest the notion of growth goals.

Growth Goals

We define *growth goals* as the moments before proficiency and beyond proficiency, for those students not there yet and for those students beyond. We can control this and plan for *all* students to at least attain proficiency and for some to move beyond proficiency in a meaningful, challenging way. This may require teachers to pause and ask themselves, "What do I do that interrupts learning and that I should stop?" It is standard practice in schools to group students largely based on one factor— their age. Think of any group of thirty people who only have their age in common. Would it be reasonable to expect all members of that group to have the same ability in mathematics; to read at the same level with the same fluency, comprehension, and vocabulary; or to have the same writing ability and produce high-level prose on any topic? Would they all demonstrate the same self-regulation in social situations? We can readily agree it would be folly to make those broad assumptions. However, this occurs routinely in classrooms. If our objective lies in the *learning*, not the *earning*, we have to focus on proficiency, not time.

Growth goals are about improving students' learning and achievement and building students' capacity to learn. Educators should commit to not interrupting any student's trajectory toward proficiency. They should plan to differentiate instruction to meet the needs of the diverse learners who populate our classrooms.

Working collaboratively to set goals, both status and growth goals, will focus dialogue on the unique and individual needs of each student. Focusing in on the student context and baseline data will drive establishment of the collective commitment and will allow for clarity on establishing the goals and the rationale for those goals. The strategies teachers choose and the professional learning they might need to become fluent in these strategies will logically flow out of this collaborative dialogue. We caution that teams take, and make, the time to do this right the first time. Rushing will minimize the impact and devalue the dialogue that can ensue when educators engage in rich discussions with their peers.

Concluding Thoughts to Heighten Systems Thinking

This chapter focused on the need for educators to *collaboratively* respond to evidence in pursuit of improved outcomes for students. It is important to remember that systems thinking leverages the skills of all adults in the building in service of all students in the building. Responding to evidence and treating data as an ally in all discussions provide the foundation for deep and intentional dialogue that will lead to meaningful benefits for students.

To tie together the main concepts of this chapter, we suggest that teams work through the reproducible "Responding to Evidence Systems Protocol" (pages 111– 113). This protocol will help you determine how well your intentions impact student achievement and growth. We intentionally highlight opportunities for teams to identify their current reality and consider areas for improvement in their practice. You may find it valuable to have team members jot down their initial thoughts individually and then bring those ideas to the team as a whole in order to ensure you hear each voice and validate each perspective. Make sure to revisit your notes and completed protocols and templates from previous chapters to guide your reflections. As you reflect on what this chapter affirmed, what you learned, and what may have given you pause, use the reproducible template "Focusing Our View Within the System: Responding to Evidence" (page 114) to acknowledge your thoughts before moving forward.

Responding to Evidence Systems Protocol

Team Members: _____ Date: _____

Unit or Topic of Study: _____

Zoom In	*Based on your current level of assessment literacy, how do you use evidence gained from assessment to adjust your instructional design?*	
	What steps have we already taken to ensure clarity of our learning intentions and success criteria across our team or department (for example, are we all clear on the level of mastery required from students)?	
	What improvements can we make in this area of our practice?	

Zoom Out	*How will our collaborative team processes and learning drive how each student receives the instruction he or she needs as he or she needs it?*	
	How does our team currently monitor the impact of our intentions relative to student learning?	
	How do we currently elicit feedback from our students regarding the impact of our: • Learning environment? • Learning styles? • Level of student choice? • Instructional agility to respond to students in the moment?	
	How do we systematically respond to the feedback we get from our students? What improvements can we make in this area of our practice?	

Panoramic	How does the manner in which we seek, gather, and discuss evidence enable us to accurately respond to that evidence?	
	What building or district resources currently exist to support our implementation of core (Tier 1) instruction?	
	What building or district resources currently exist to support our ability to differentiate or provide supplemental instruction?	
	What improvements can we make in this area of our practice?	

Focusing Our View Within the System:
Responding to Evidence

Zoom In	Zoom Out
What is our current reality? What kind of information are we looking for to move us toward the results we desire?	Why do we need this information? How will it advance our work?
Panoramic	**View From Above**
How will these decisions or conversations impact our system? What is the potential to create greater balance and alignment within?	How will we leverage the gifts and talents of the people within the system to heighten systems thinking throughout?

CHAPTER 6

EMBEDDING EVIDENCE-BASED PRACTICES IN LEARNING ORGANIZATIONS

Every member of the educational community is a leader. While some roles are formalized with a title, there are many important aspects of leadership that apply to all members of the school community.

—Tom Hierck

Fisher and Frey (2015) highlight the importance of embedding a systems approach into daily practice. This final chapter highlights some evidence-based practices we have personally found effective for leaders and teams. We apply these practices in our own careers, in facilitative work with other schools, and in ongoing efforts to explore new options to raise the achievement results for all students. The evidence of effectiveness is based on our personal experiences as educators except where otherwise cited throughout this chapter.

- **Zoom in:** What is our current reality with embedding evidence-based practices, and how can I support the achievement of our collective goals?

- **Zoom out:** How does the organization support our collective learning in order to advance the system?

- **Panoramic:** How consistently do we monitor, uphold, and reflect on the current priorities to support the differentiated needs of the adult learners within the organization? What evidence do we use to track whether our intentions translate to high levels of impact relative to improved student achievement?

Embedding Evidence-Based Practices as Leaders

Schools need leadership from all members of the school community. When it comes time to lead crucial conversations about assessment practice and embed the right work in daily practice, the formal leaders will need others to step forward. In this section, we will first examine who can become leaders and what leaders do that makes them successful. We will then discuss specific evidence-based practices that leaders should engage in to ensure success for the whole team.

Determining Who Are Leaders

We work with leaders in schools all across the United States and Canada. Here's what we know—they don't all have formalized titles! Although we have spoken of the need for school and district leaders to make their presence known and be active participants in embedding a systems approach within schools, it would be folly to suggest leadership can, or should, only emanate from those positions. As Fullan (2014) indicates:

> The principal does not lead all instructional learning. The principal does work to ensure that intense instructional focus and continuous learning are the core work of the school, and does this by being a talent scout and social engineer, building a culture for learning, tapping others to co-lead, and, well, basically being a learning leader for all. (p. 90)

All educators have the attributes of developing expectations, communicating, being present, participating in learning, engaging with others, and committing to the ongoing growth of the leadership skills available and accessible to them. Principals are not the exclusive leaders in a school. In fact, the principals we encounter in successful schools have often learned the value of leadership that many individuals display across the system in pursuit of a collective commitment. Leadership moves schools forward. Leadership is about the choices you make, not the seat you occupy.

John Maxwell (2011) states that "99 percent of all leadership occurs not from the top but from the middle of an organization" (p. 1). He goes on to suggest that leaders in the middle can do five things to develop a positive attitude about their contributions.

1. **Develop strong relationships with key people:** Building relationships with others is more important and more fulfilling than competing with them.

2. **Define a win in terms of teamwork:** Don't lose sight of the fact that one person—either a team member or a leader—is not responsible for the success of an entire team. Team members and leaders create success together.

3. **Engage in continual communication:** Keep leaders informed of the work that's occurring toward realizing the team's vision, and communicate with

them to receive feedback and ask for information you need to share with
the team.

4. **Gain experience and maturity:** Accepting responsibility and working to
gain experience over time makes for strong team members.

5. **Put the team above your personal success:** Foregoing personal gains for
the good of the team is necessary for success in high-stakes situations.

Peter Drucker (1996) suggests four simple leadership characteristics:

1. The only definition of a *leader* is someone who has *followers*.
   Some people are thinkers. Some are prophets. Both roles are
   important and badly needed. But without followers, there can
   be no leaders.

2. An effective leader is not someone who is loved or admired.
   He or she is someone whose followers do the right things.
   Popularity is not leadership. *Results* are.

3. Leaders are highly visible. They therefore set *examples*.

4. Leadership is not rank, privileges, titles, or money. It is
   responsibility. (p. xii)

In other words, schools and districts have many potential leaders, and they clearly
have lots of opportunities to exercise this leadership. Rather than just looking at the
requisite skill set and matching people with certain skills to fill a certain need, the
culture sets conditions where individuals feel comfortable (and safe and supported)
stepping forward and sharing their expertise. James Kouzes and Barry Posner (2010)
suggest that leadership capacity is "broadly distributed in the population, and it's
accessible to anyone who has passion and purpose to change the way things are"
(p. 5). It's fair to conclude that our best teachers actively lead and our best leaders
engage in teaching. This balance allows educators in schools to invest their time in
those activities that move in the direction of desired outcomes.

Identifying Attributes of a Leader

In nurturing the leadership talent that resides in every school, it helps to have some
clarity about desired attributes. Lyle Kirtman (2014) describes these attributes as
competencies, and he defines *competency* as "an observable behavior that demonstrates
skills, learning, and experience" (p. 5). His seven leadership competencies are more
than just a list of commonly known characteristics, as he has derived them from his
work with more than three hundred school districts and more than one thousand
educational leaders. We believe schools have the skills identified in abundance, and
you will find these skills crucial in helping define the outcomes of a quality assessment
plan at your school. Kirtman (2014) identifies the following seven competencies for
a leader.

1. **Challenges the status quo:** This relates to having less focus on rule following and compliance but does not mean simply breaking or ignoring the rules. It does mean starting with a focus on the desired results. In our assessment dialogue, this means staying aware of external exams' (such as those from Smarter Balanced Assessment Consortium [SBAC] and Partnership for Assessment of Readiness for College and Careers [PARCC]) demands but not being overtly driven by them. The worst way to prepare a student for a test that covers everything is to try to teach everything. "Depth over breadth" is our axiom.

2. **Builds trust through clear communications and expectations:** This focuses on leaders' ability to influence and motivate others through clear communications and expectations. These individuals value effective collaboration and develop trust and confidence with their teammates to achieve results. Leaders create clarity around the purpose of assessment as a source of evidence rather than a source of ranking.

3. **Creates a commonly owned plan for success:** A written plan for success is created with a systemic focus on the school and the school system. It focuses on teams investing in the implementation effort. The shift in assessment practice resides in the doing, not in the talking.

4. **Focuses on team over self:** The notion here is that leaders are only as good as the strengths of the people around them. They give credit to the team instead of highlighting individual performances. They know that they do not own all the best ideas, and they understand the power of collective expertise. Team members meet to discuss the results of all students, not just their individual students' results.

5. **Has a high sense of urgency for change and sustainable results in improving student achievement:** Leaders place their focus on action and fast movement on key issues to quickly solve problems. The work focuses on shared purpose as a means to improve results. When results improve or lag, leaders know why. The key to improving is to know the causes and effects of sound practice.

6. **Commits to continuous improvement:** Leaders direct energy toward always trying to improve and toward exploring new ideas and practices. Within their collaborative teams, they understand the value of using data to inform their practice. Until all students achieve the desired results, they do not consider the work complete.

7. **Builds external networks and partnerships:** Leaders recognize the importance of reaching beyond the school walls to form partnerships, access

new ideas, and solve problems with others. If assessment results indicate students need additional services beyond the class or school, leaders don't hesitate to pursue them.

Skilled leaders may not excel in all these competencies; however, they do practice almost all of them. Leaders understand that they must continually improve, and they realize that they can never master all these competencies, as contexts change and practices must adjust.

Leading Through Presence

Where leaders spend their time is significant. If leaders expect certain work to be important and meaningful, then leaders make time to be present for it. They are present not just in the physical sense of attendance but in the sense that they actively engage in the dialogue, planning, frustrations, and resolutions. It means clearly committing to the purpose established by the faculty's collective will and skill. Fisher and Frey (2015) identify the importance of presence across learning environments and speak to being present in the classroom, in professional development, in a professional learning community, and on learning walks (loosely structured classroom observations carried out by groups of teachers). From an assessment perspective, we would add the importance of presence in data team conversations, RTI work, and individualized education program (IEP) or behavior education program (BEP) formation. Let's look at each of these additions through the lens of presence. The leader's role in all of these cases is their presence (attending the meetings). While they cannot be as fluent as their teachers in any of these areas, their presence will allow them access to the meeting information and allow them to ask higher-level questions.

Data Teams

As mentioned in chapter 5, data teams engage in essential dialogue on assessment evidence. Leaders' presence in these conversations helps highlight all the elements of effective collaboration, keeps the focus on results, sharpens the expectation that all students will attain proficiency, and reminds the team that responsibility for the desired results rests with educators.

RTI

Presence in the essential work that underpins RTI requires all participants to engage in the dialogue as they look for solutions to the needs the team has identified from the assessment evidence. The notion of *all* students has critical importance in these conversations as educators recognize that not all students will reach the same goals at the same time.

IEPs and BEPs

An *individualized education program* is a written document that outlines the educational program designed to meet a child's individual needs. Every child who receives special education services must have an IEP. Teacher teams can create IEPs for students who are behind in their academic progression or who are lacking in basic, foundational skills. The IEP has two general purposes: (1) to set learning goals for the student, and (2) to delineate the services that the school or district will provide for the student. A *behavior education program* is a support system for students who do not respond to core supports. The teacher, a parent, or another connected adult can refer students to the BEP if they need increased behavioral support. The BEP aims to prevent students from engaging in severe problem behavior. The effectiveness of the BEP lies in responding early, before behaviors get so entrenched that remediation becomes protracted. Teachers must intervene when students start to exhibit more off-task behavior, when they still have the opportunity to connect back to the desired outcomes. Teachers have committed to all students, even those most off task, and staying present in this case means engaging in solution seeking, not consequence making.

Ponder Box

As you consider how to activate leadership in your building or organization, how can the attributes of a leader now guide the manner in which you elevate others to carry the torch with you? How will you utilize presence to lead by example and with purpose?

Embedding Evidence-Based Practices as Teams

It is important that teams embed evidence-based practice in daily instruction and assessment design. This becomes even more powerful when teams can link it across content areas, ensuring that students understand the relevance of the desired outcomes. In this section, we will focus on evidence-based practices teams should incorporate into their instruction, such as identifying best practices and setting expectations and goals, as well as evidence-based practices teams should incorporate into their collaborative work, including having one conversation at a time and making time.

Identifying Best Practices

We have engaged colleagues in this process, and inevitably, two questions emerge at the outset: (1) What works? and (2) How do you know? If you intend to make this common practice, those are two critical questions. For a research-based response to both these questions, we return to the work of Hattie (2009), who has examined research related to more than 150 teaching strategies to look at their impact on student learning. Without digressing into a lengthy statistical description, we will say Hattie indicates that a typical year of teaching produces an effect size of 0.4 of a standard deviation, translating into twelve months of academic growth. He further suggests that educators ought to look at practices that go beyond the effect size of 0.4 to substantially impact student outcomes. In the assessment domain, the following practices (with their effect sizes in parentheses) have significance.

- Student self-reported grades (1.44)

- Response to intervention (1.07)

- Formative assessment (0.90)

- Feedback (0.75)

- Teacher clarity (0.75)

Because 0.4 of a standard deviation equates to twelve months' growth in academic terms, this means the preceding practices identified almost double that growth in some areas, and even exceed twofold growth in others. From a practical, school-based or classroom-based perspective, it is critical that teachers monitor progress of the chosen strategies' impact. If you have evidence that a practice works, our advice is simple—keep doing it! It's the evidence that is the crucial need. Let's not confuse best practice with the practice you do best—they might not be the same thing. Evidence from high-quality assessments will ensure that you know which of your inputs into the learning process have positive outputs in terms of student performance.

Setting Expectations and Goals

After completing a twenty-page paper for a university course, Tom's daughter eagerly awaited the result. When she did receive it, she felt completely dismayed by the letter *B* that appeared on the cover page and the word *vague* written underneath it. She found no other comment on the remaining pages. After she met with her professor, the grade changed to an A simply because she went to see him. She did not intend for that to happen. She wanted to know what she needed to do to produce a high-quality paper. She needed the expectations clarified so she could set her goals. We are certain that many readers of this book have had personal school experiences that resemble Tom's daughter's. In the absence of this clarity, students can only guess what the teacher wants, produce the best effort (in their minds at least), and hope they won the teacher lottery—that is, they have landed the teacher whose unstated expectations align with their best effort at completion. There is a better way. Fisher and Frey (2015) suggest educators can reduce task frustration by tending to the following five tips that they have adapted from Wayne Madden's (2014) business-world work.

1. Be clear about what you want.

2. Ask for clarifying questions up front.

3. Avoid managing the *how*.

4. Assist in removing obstructions and overcoming obstacles.

5. Manage the outcomes.

Hattie (2012) has analyzed methods teachers try in classrooms to positively impact student learning. He speaks to the need for teachers to develop learning intentions and success criteria as crucial in targeting the learning to the desired outcomes. *Learning intentions* identify what teachers expect students to learn from the lesson, whereas *success criteria* become the way of knowing that the learning has been achieved. For example, a second-grade mathematics class could have the learning intention, "We are learning about place value in numbers up to 10,000." The success criterion could be, "I can explain the place value of digits in a number" or "I can read, write, and order numbers." This clarity makes the goal visible and allows both teacher and student to monitor the progress toward proficiency. Hattie (2012) suggests, "Learning intentions describe what it is that we want students to learn and their clarity is at the heart of formative assessment" (p. 53). If teachers unclearly communicate what they want students to learn or what the endpoint of the learning looks like, they cannot possibly expect to design a quality assessment item or for it to yield some valuable insight. Hattie (2012) defines *success criteria* as "knowledge of end points—that is, how do we know when we arrive?" (p. 56). Students may get involved in designing the success criteria with teachers, and the key is to get them engaged in the learning and to enjoy the challenge that comes with acquiring new knowledge.

In developing the notion of learning intentions and success criteria, Hattie (2012) outlines five important components.

1. **Challenge:** This should not appear so difficult as to seem unattainable but should appear that a pathway to proficiency seems possible from the student's starting point.

2. **Commitment:** This refers to the determination to reach a goal; the greater the commitment, the better the outcome.

3. **Confidence:** This refers to the belief that the student can attain the goal.

4. **Student expectations:** Students have accurate understanding of their levels of achievement.

5. **Conceptual understanding:** This comes as a result of students acquiring both surface and deep understanding.

These five components are crucial to assessment design—creating tools that yield evidence of student learning—and will be integral in setting goals, both by the teacher and the student. To review how a teacher applied Hattie's components, visit **go.SolutionTree.com/assessment** to access the reproducible "Cowichan Valley School District Goal-Setting Example," which includes a vignette of one teacher's experience with goal setting and sample artifacts.

Having One Conversation at a Time

One frequent misunderstanding of common formative assessment work is the notion that this simply means that a group of teachers at a grade level in a content area give the same test. The reality is more complex. The challenging part occurs after the test, when teachers need to sit down and discuss the results. Consider this: How often does your leadership team reflect on how its work contributes to or hinders progress toward achievement of the system's goals? Do all stakeholders understand the vision and how to effectively advance it? Or, do you sometimes get ahead of yourselves and—unfortunately—get too far ahead of the work instead of walking alongside others to get the desired results? Engaging in one conversation at a time enables us to build one voice around the *why*, *what*, and *how* of our Unstoppable Assessment systems work.

As we emphasized previously, the strength of the relationships on your team and the trust you have in each other will impact that very first data conversation you have. Even the strongest teams will struggle. This principle holds true for leaders at all levels of the organization. If we have effectively built trust and determined norms for our collaborative work together, then we become more comfortable with showing vulnerability and asking for help when we struggle.

Making Time

Perhaps the single biggest lament heard in schools is, "We don't have time for anything else. Our plate is full!" Let's be clear—we believe that time is the most precious resource in schools. How individual teachers and faculties decide how to use their time speaks to the things those teachers and faculties value most. A day does, indeed, have a finite number of hours. If you consider something a priority, you will make time for it. We can't think of a more noble priority than ensuring all students get to mastery on the essential learning. This basic student right will set them up to become productive members of their communities.

Ponder Box

Elevating individuals within your building or organization develops a critical mass of leaders who will help you champion the systems work. What skill sets do you currently model that can help these individuals create systems thinking teams? What skill sets might you begin to develop? Who can you learn from to support your efforts?

Concluding Thoughts to Heighten Systems Thinking

Schools are complex, intertwined organizations reminiscent of Russian Matryoshka dolls, which have the smallest doll nested inside increasingly larger dolls. Your classroom system (and its complexities) nests itself inside a grade-level, multigrade-level, or departmental system, which nests itself in a school system nested in a district system. Each system is impacted by and impacts the others. It's critical that information and evidence flow through these systems largely unimpeded, not subjected to chain-of-command roles that dictate who can lead. Leadership in the assessment realm has to include all school members, including our students.

This chapter has introduced aspects of embedding evidence-based practices as we build an Unstoppable Assessment system. To tie together the main concepts of this chapter, we suggest that teams work through the reproducible "Embedding Evidence-Based Practices Systems Protocol" (pages 125–126). Effective assessment practice has the capacity to impact all students' outcomes and will strengthen all teachers' instructional practice. Working as a system ensures the flow of information, and evidence will emphasize the strength of this work. As you reflect on what this chapter affirmed, what you learned, and what may have given you pause, use the reproducible template "Focusing Our View Within the System: Embedding Evidence-Based Practices" (page 127) to acknowledge your thoughts before moving forward.

Embedding Evidence-Based Practices Systems Protocol

Team Members: _____ Date: _____

Unit or Topic of Study: _____

Zoom In	*What is our current reality with embedding evidence-based practices, and how am I able to support the achievement of our collective goals?*	
	What do I understand to be the current priorities within our organization?	
	How do my personal growth goals also support a contribution to those organizational priorities?	
Zoom Out	*How does the organization support our collective learning in order to advance the system forward?*	
	How does the implementation of our professional learning community framework (common understanding of purpose, time for collaboration, opportunities to develop and revise assessment and instructional experiences) enable me to work toward the achievement of those priorities?	
	Where are the opportunities for improvement in this area of my practice?	

page 1 of 2

Panoramic	*How consistently do we monitor, uphold, and reflect on the current priorities to support the differentiated needs of the adult learners within the organization?*
	What evidence do we use to track whether our intentions translate to high levels of impact relative to improved student achievement?

Focusing Our View Within the System: Embedding Evidence-Based Practices

Zoom In	Zoom Out
What is our current reality? What kind of information are we looking for to move us toward the results we desire?	Why do we need this information? How will it advance our work?
Panoramic	**View From Above**
How will these decisions or conversations impact our system? What is the potential to create greater balance and alignment within?	How will we leverage the gifts and talents of the people within the system to heighten systems thinking throughout?

Assessing Unstoppable Learning © 2018 Solution Tree Press • SolutionTree.com
Visit **go.SolutionTree.com/assessment** to download this free reproducible.

Championing the Work:
Dream, Design, Do, and Discover

We hope that, having read this book, you now feel better prepared to dream the dream that all students will reach their highest level and that you and your teammates have the foundational knowledge to get them there. The circumstances students face do not determine their endpoint; they just determine our starting point. Collectively, we help students plot the course.

This book endeavored to identify the mindset behind the key work of assessment as much as the skills of effective assessment practice. The four key principles of systems thinking: (1) relationships, (2) communication, (3) responsiveness, and (4) sustainability—are linked intentionally and must all be present to maximize teams' capacity to function with a systems view. We believe we have armed you to design such an assessment plan. Whether through building on these four principles or working through steps to make the elements of Unstoppable Assessment a reality in your collaborative work, teams will move forward with high-quality assessments that generate evidence to inform your course of action or next steps.

We want you to consider not just *what* the work involves but *how* you plan for it and approach it in a way where your entire team comes together and leaves no one behind. Teams recognize that having individuals at different levels of readiness is *not* the problem, provided each team member commits to growth. This forms the *do* phase of the work, and it truly requires all hands on deck. We do not know of any school that achieved its best through the work of individuals. We encourage you to avoid creating what Williams and Hierck (2015) refer to as *pockets of excellence*. Let's create schools and districts of excellence where all adults work in concert with all students.

We've collected the panoramic questions that appear throughout this book and compiled them into one sheet for easy access and reflection (see the reproducible "Panoramic Questions," page 131). We ask that you revisit these questions and consider the components of your road map—and the timing of your messaging—

while recognizing that each team reading this book will start at a different place in the journey. We have permission to be where we are. If we are not in the place we desire, however, we cannot continue to stay there. This work is about you, your team, and how you collectively create the next page in your story. It's also about using effective assessment strategies to ensure *all* students achieve at the highest levels and graduate armed with significantly more skills, greater capacity, and more belief in the impact they can have moving forward.

We hope this book has taken you on a journey of discovery—discovery of the special and unique talents that reside in all your colleagues (and yourself), discovery of the success stories yet to be told that reside in your students, and discovery that the key to unprecedented levels of success begins with establishing a collective commitment and taking that first step together. As we conclude this part of our learning together, we encourage you to stay the course. Learn as a team so you can rise together.

We know that you will have a tremendous impact.

Panoramic Questions

Chapter	Panoramic Question	Your Notes or Ideas to Advance This Work
Chapter 1	How might we seek, gather, discuss, and respond to evidence from our stakeholders that we are building trust and that positive adult relationships are strengthening the intended outcomes of our work as an organization?	
Chapter 2	What is the connection between creating a common scope and sequence across the team and building a guaranteed and viable curriculum for students?	
Chapter 3	How will we prepare to report our evidence in order to efficiently discuss it with our colleagues and our students?	
Chapter 4	What additional information or resources do we need now as a result of our evidence-based discussion? What is our next step as a result of our learning during our evidence-based discussion?	
Chapter 5	How does the manner in which we seek, gather, and discuss evidence enable us to accurately respond to that evidence?	
Chapter 6	How consistently do we monitor, uphold, and reflect on the current priorities to support the differentiated needs of the adult learners within the organization? What evidence do we use to track whether our intentions translate to high levels of impact relative to improved student achievement?	

References and Resources

Ainsworth, L. (2003). *Power standards: Identifying the standards that matter the most.* Denver: Advanced Learning Press.

Ainsworth, L. (2011). *Rigorous curriculum design.* Englewood, CO: Lead + Learn Press.

Ainsworth, L., & Viegut, D. (2006). *Common formative assessments: How to connect standards-based instruction and assessment.* Thousand Oaks, CA: Corwin Press.

Anderson, L. W., & Krathwohl, D. (Eds.). (2001). *A taxonomy for learning, teaching, and assessing: A revision of Bloom's taxonomy of educational objectives.* Boston: Allyn & Bacon.

Bailey, K., & Jakicic, C. (2012). *Common formative assessment: A toolkit for Professional Learning Communities at Work.* Bloomington, IN: Solution Tree Press.

Bailey, K., Jakicic, C., & Spiller, J. (2014). *Collaborating for success with the Common Core: A toolkit for Professional Learning Communities at Work.* Bloomington, IN: Solution Tree Press.

Bloom, B. S. (Ed.). (1956). *Taxonomy of educational objectives: The classification of educational goals; Handbook I: Cognitive domain.* New York: David McKay.

Bryk, A. S., Sebring, P. B., Allensworth, E., Luppescu, S., & Easton, J. Q. (2010). *Organizing schools for improvement: Lessons from Chicago.* Chicago: University of Chicago Press.

Buffum, A., Mattos, M., & Weber, C. (2009). *Pyramid response to intervention: RTI, professional learning communities, and how to respond when kids don't learn.* Bloomington, IN: Solution Tree Press.

Burke, K. (2010). *Balanced assessment: From formative to summative.* Bloomington, IN: Solution Tree Press.

Chapman, C., & Vagle, N. D. (2011). *Motivating students: 25 strategies to light the fire of engagement.* Bloomington, IN: Solution Tree Press.

Covey, S. M. R. (2006). *The speed of trust: The one thing that changes everything.* New York: Free Press.

Drucker, P. F. (1996). Foreword. In F. Hesselbein, M. Goldsmith, & R. Beckhard (Eds.), *The leader of the future* (pp. xi–xvi). San Francisco: Jossey-Bass.

DuFour, R., DuFour, R., Eaker, R., & Many, T. W. (2010). *Learning by doing: A handbook for Professional Learning Communities at Work* (2nd ed.). Bloomington, IN: Solution Tree Press.

DuFour, R., DuFour, R., Eaker, R., Many, T. W., & Mattos, M. (2016). *Learning by doing: A handbook for Professional Learning Communities at Work* (3rd ed.). Bloomington, IN: Solution Tree Press.

Erkens, C. (2016). *Collaborative common assessments: Teamwork. Instruction. Results.* Bloomington, IN: Solution Tree Press.

Erkens, C., Schimmer, T., & Vagle, N. D. (2017). *Essential assessment: Six tenets for bringing hope, efficacy, and achievement to the classroom.* Bloomington, IN: Solution Tree Press.

Fisher, D., & Frey, N. (2015). *Unstoppable learning: Seven essential elements to unleash student potential.* Bloomington, IN: Solution Tree Press.

Fullan, M. (2005). *Leadership and sustainability: System thinkers in action.* Thousand Oaks, CA: Corwin Press.

Fullan, M. (2014). *The principal: Three keys to maximizing impact.* San Francisco: Jossey-Bass.

Fullan, M., & Quinn, J. (2016). *Coherence: The right drivers in action for schools, districts, and systems.* Thousand Oaks, CA: Corwin Press.

Graham, P., & Ferriter, W. M. (2010). *Building a Professional Learning Community at Work: A guide to the first year.* Bloomington, IN: Solution Tree Press.

Guskey, T. R. (2015). *On your mark: Challenging the conventions of grading and reporting.* Bloomington, IN: Solution Tree Press.

Hattie, J. (2003, October). *Teachers make a difference: What is the research evidence?* Paper presented at the Building Teacher Quality: What Does the Research Tell Us? ACER Research Conference, Melbourne, Australia. Accessed at http://research.acer.edu.au/cgi/viewcontent.cgi?article=1003 &context=research_conference_2003 on January 25, 2017.

Hattie, J. (2009). *Visible learning: A synthesis of over 800 meta-analyses relating to achievement.* New York: Routledge.

Hattie, J. (2012). *Visible learning for teachers: Maximizing impact on learning.* New York: Routledge.

Hierck, T., & Weber, C. (2014). *RTI roadmap for school leaders: Plan and go.* Englewood, CO: Lead + Learn Press.

Hoy, W. K., & Tschannen-Moran, M. (2003). The conceptualization and measurement of faculty trust in schools: The omnibus T-scale. In W. Hoy & C. Miskel (Eds.), *Studies in leading and organizing schools* (pp. 181–208). Greenwich, CT: Information Age.

Hussar, W. J., & Bailey, T. M. (2014). *Projections of education statistics to 2022* (41st ed.) (NCES 2014-051). Washington, DC: U.S. Department of education, National Center for Education Statistics. Accessed at https://nces.ed.gov/pubs2014/2014051.pdf on June 8, 2017.

Jacobs, H. H., & Johnson, A. (2009). *The curriculum mapping planner: Templates, tools, and resources for effective professional development.* Alexandria, VA: Association for Supervision and Curriculum Development.

Katzenbach, J. R., & Smith, D. K. (1993). The discipline of teams. *Harvard Business Review, 71*(2), 111–120.

Kirtman, L. (2014). *Leadership and teams: The missing piece of the educational reform puzzle.* Boston: Pearson.

Kouzes, J. M., & Posner, B. Z. (2010). *The truth about leadership: The no-fads, heart-of-the-matter facts you need to know*. San Francisco: Jossey-Bass.

Lenz, B. (2015). *Transforming schools using project-based learning, performance assessment, and Common Core standards*. San Francisco: Jossey-Bass.

Madden, W. (2014, May 1). *Management 101: Set clear expectations*. Accessed at https://omhub .wordpress.com/2014/05/01/management-101-set-clear-expectations on October 16, 2014.

Marzano, R. J. (2003). *What works in schools: Translating research into action*. Alexandria, VA: Association for Supervision and Curriculum Development.

Maxwell, J. C. (2011). *The 360° leader: Developing your influence from anywhere in the organization*. Nashville, TN: Thomas Nelson.

McDowell, M. (2017). *Rigorous PBL by design: Three shifts for developing confident and competent learners*. Thousand Oaks, CA: Corwin Press.

McLaughlin, M. W., & Talbert, J. E. (2006). *Building school-based teacher learning communities: Professional strategies to improve student achievement*. New York: Teachers College Press.

Monahan, M. B. (2013, February 16). *Persuasive vs. argument writing*. Accessed at www.vriuvm.org /uncategorized/persuasive-vs-argument-writing on January 25, 2017.

National Governors Association Center for Best Practices & Council of Chief State School Officers. (2010). *Common Core State Standards for English language arts and literacy in history/social studies, science, and technical subjects*. Washington, DC: Authors. Accessed at www .corestandards.org/assets/CCSSI_ELA%20Standards.pdf on January 25, 2017.

Nottingham, J. (2017). *Learning pit*. Accessed at www.jamesnottingham.co.uk/learning-pit on June 6, 2017.

Nuthall, G. (2007). *The hidden lives of learners*. Wellington, New Zealand: NZCER Press.

Odden, A. R., & Archibald, S. J. (2009). *Doubling student performance . . . and finding the resources to do it*. Thousand Oaks, CA: Corwin Press.

Papert, S. A. (1998, June 2). *Child power: Keys to the new learning of the digital century*. Paper presented at the 11th Colin Cherry Memorial Lecture on Communication, London, England.

Partnership for 21st Century Learning. (n.d.). *The 4Cs research series*. Accessed at www.p21.org/our -work/4cs-research-series on January 25, 2017.

Posner, G. (2004). *Analyzing the curriculum* (3rd ed.). New York: McGraw-Hill.

Reeves, D. (2002). *The leader's guide to standards: A blueprint for educational equity and excellence*. San Francisco: Jossey-Bass.

Reeves, D. (Ed.). (2007). *Ahead of the curve: The power of assessment to transform teaching and learning*. Bloomington, IN: Solution Tree Press.

Reeves, D. (2010). *Transforming professional development into student results*. Alexandria, VA: Association for Supervision and Curriculum Development.

Schimmer, T. (2016). *Grading from the inside out: Bringing accuracy to student assessment through a standards-based mindset*. Bloomington, IN: Solution Tree Press.

Schmoker, M. (1999). *Results: The key to continuous school improvement* (2nd ed.). Alexandria, VA: Association for Supervision and Curriculum Development.

Schmoker, M. (2006). *Results now: How we can achieve unprecedented improvements in teaching and learning.* Alexandria, VA: Association for Supervision and Curriculum Development.

Schmoker, M. (2011). *Focus: Elevating the essentials to radically improve student learning.* Alexandria, VA: Association for Supervision and Curriculum Development.

SciMathMN & Minnesota Department of Education. (n.d.). *Framework for the Minnesota science and mathematics standards.* Accessed at www.scimathmn.org/stemtc on January 25, 2017.

Senge, P. M. (1990). *The fifth discipline: The art and practice of the learning organization.* New York: Doubleday/Currency.

Shepard, L. A. (2000). The role of assessment in a learning culture. *Educational Researcher, 29*(7), 4–14.

Stephenson, S. (2009). *Leading with trust: How to build strong school teams.* Bloomington, IN: Solution Tree Press.

Stiggins, R. J., Arter, J. A., Chappuis, J., & Chappuis, S. (2004). *Classroom assessment for student learning: Doing it right—using it well.* Portland, OR: Assessment Training Institute.

Stillwater Area Public Schools. (n.d.). *Assessments and learning analytics.* Accessed at www.stillwater.k12.mn.us/teaching-learning/assessment-and-evaluation on January 25, 2017.

Tomlinson, C. (2014). *The differentiated classroom: Responding to the needs of all learners* (2nd ed.). Alexandria, VA: Association for Supervision and Curriculum Development.

Tschannen-Moran, M., & Hoy, W. K. (2000). A multidisciplinary analysis of the nature, meaning, and measurement of trust. *Review of Educational Research, 70*(4), 547–593.

Vagle, N. D. (2015). *Design in five: Essential phases to create engaging assessment practice.* Bloomington, IN: Solution Tree Press.

Wellman, B., & Lipton, L. (2004). *Data-driven dialogue: A facilitator's guide to collaborative inquiry.* Sherman, CT: MiraVia.

Wiggins, G., & McTighe, J. (2005). *Understanding by design* (2nd ed.). Alexandria, VA: Association for Supervision and Curriculum Development.

Wiliam, D., & Leahy, S. (2015). *Embedding formative assessment: Practical techniques for K–12 classrooms.* West Palm Beach, FL: Learning Sciences International.

Williams, K. C., & Hierck, T. (2015). *Starting a movement: Building culture from the inside out in professional learning communities.* Bloomington, IN: Solution Tree Press.

Index

Unstoppable Learning
Douglas Fisher and Nancy Frey
Discover proven methods to enhance teaching and learning schoolwide. Identify questions educators should ask to guarantee a positive classroom culture where students learn from each other, not just teachers. Explore ways to adapt teaching in response to students' individual needs.
BKF662

Adapting Unstoppable Learning
Yazmin Pineda Zapata and Rebecca Brooks
This practical guide expands on the Unstoppable Learning model to explore accessible learning for students with varying needs, from physical disabilities to twice-exceptionality. Forms, tools, and diagrams designed to aid instructional planning are also included.
BKF734

Seven Keys to a Positive Learning Environment in Your Classroom
Tom Hierck
Creating a positive classroom learning environment is a complex but necessary task. By following the seven keys the author outlines, teachers can establish clearer expectations, enhance instruction and assessment practices, and foster quality relationships with students, maximizing the potential of all students.
BKF721

Simplifying Common Assessment
Kim Bailey and Chris Jakicic
Discover how to develop effective and efficient assessments. The authors simplify assessment development to give teacher teams the confidence to write and use team-designed common formative assessments that help ensure all students master essential skills and concepts.
BKF750

"Excellent engagement
in what truly matters
in **assessment**.

Great examples!"

—Carol Johnson, superintendent,
Central Dauphin School District, Pennsylvania

 PD Services

Our experts draw from decades of research and their own experiences to bring you
practical strategies for designing and implementing quality assessments. You can choose
from a range of customizable services, from a one-day overview to a multiyear process.

Book your assessment PD today!
888.763.9045

Solution Tree